AF471249

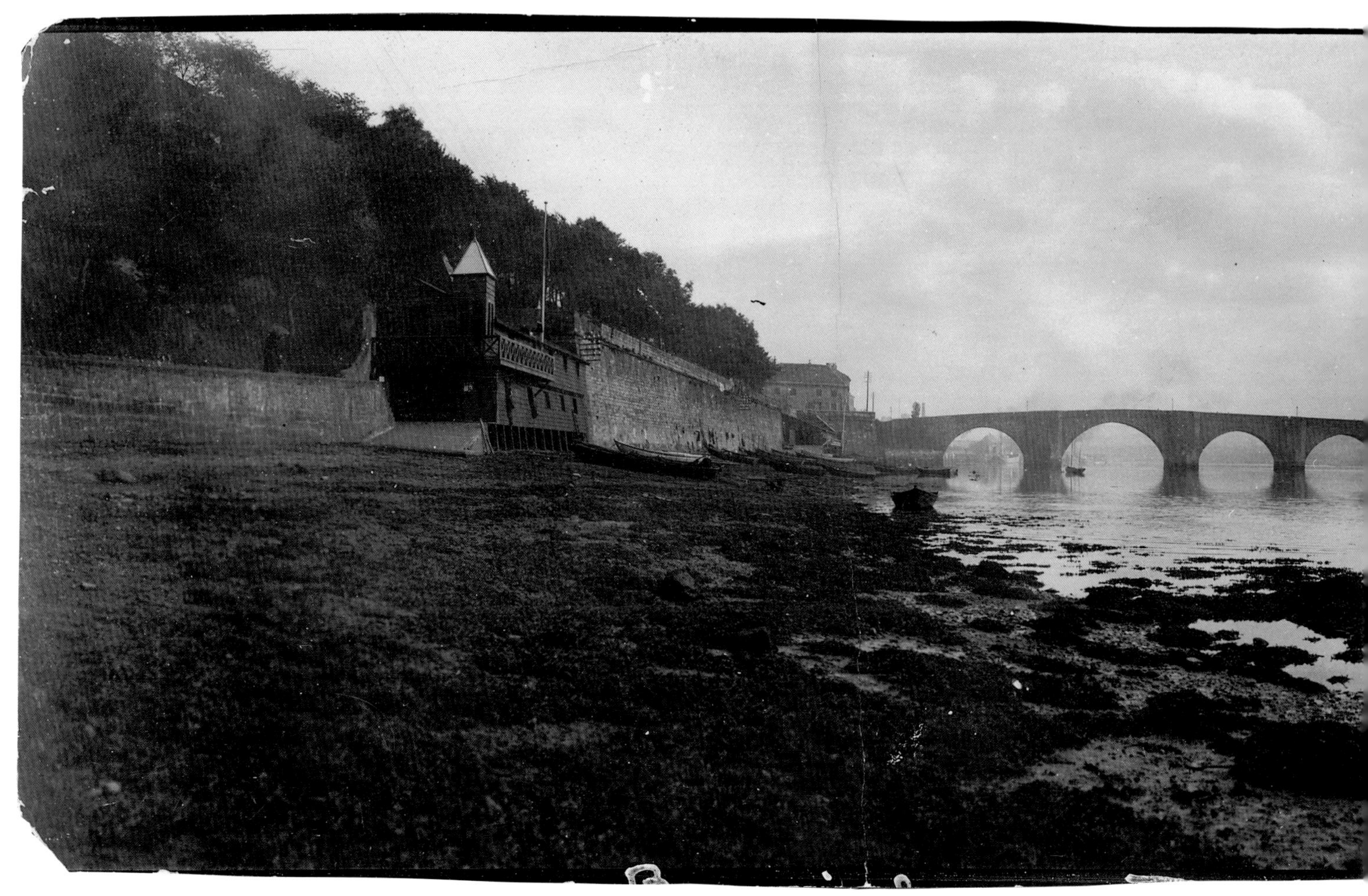

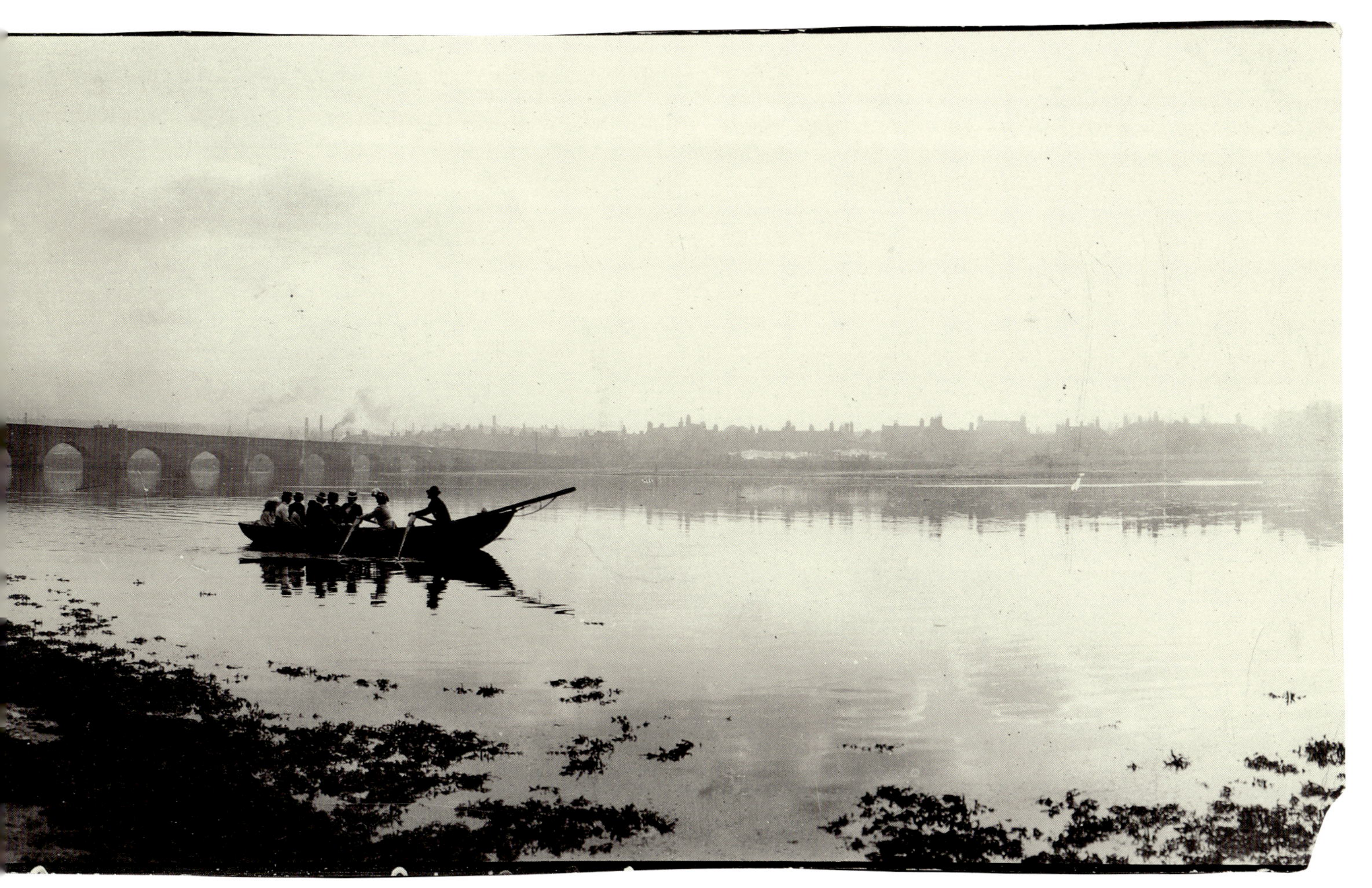

All Human Life:
Great Photographs
from the
Hulton Deutsch Collection

Bruce Bernard

Published January 1994 in an edition of 2,000 copies
on the occasion of Barbican Art Gallery's exhibition

**All Human Life: Great Photographs from
the Hulton Deutsch Collection**

ISBN 0 946372 31 4

Exhibition selected by Bruce Bernard,
assisted by Sue Percival

Exhibition organised by
Brigitte Lardinois and Jane Alison, Barbican Art Gallery
Sue Percival, the Hulton Deutsch Collection

Designed by Derek Birdsall R.D.I., Omnific

Printed in Great Britain by Balding + Mansell

All photographs in the exhibition and this accompanying
book are owned by the Hulton Deutsch Collection

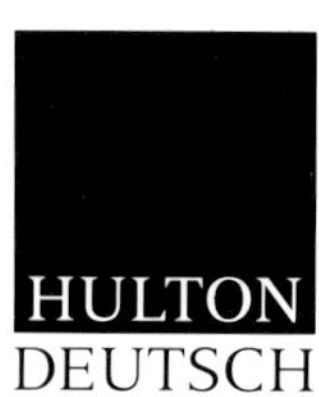

Contents

Acknowledgements

Barbican Art Gallery acknowledges with grateful thanks
the following for their support of *All Human Life*:

 Apple Computer U.K. Limited

REUTERS

XDRA Publishing

ILFORD Photo

Barbican Art Gallery would like to thank its
Corporate Members

3i Group plc
Barings Group
Bethlem Royal and Maudsley Hospitals
British Gas North Thames
British Petroleum Company p.l.c.
British Telecommunications plc
Levi's Red Tab Jeans
Nomura International
Norddeutsche Landesbank
Robert Fleming Holdings Ltd
Save & Prosper plc
Sun Alliance Group
TSB Group plc
Unilever plc
S.G. Warburg plc

Foreword

Photography is surely the most direct visual medium that the human race has invented in order to capture and communicate its own existence, and our exhibition *All Human Life* has been created to convey some of life's realities and passions with all the vividness and immediacy found in the countless photographic images now happily preserved in a single and unique archive.

It has been a little celebrated fact that one of the largest photographic archives in the world exists in West London where immediacy can be found on every shelf. Although the original BBC Hulton Picture Library was never conceived and amassed as a coherent collection in the curatorial sense, the importance of its colossal archive and the extraordinary wealth of its material never fails to impress all who come into contact with it. Under its new title of the Hulton Deutsch Collection, it engenders a passion for photography that seems to be shared by everyone who uses the collection and this has certainly been the case with all those involved with the effort to create this major showing at Barbican Art Gallery. Now, we hope, that enthusiasm can be experienced by everyone viewing the *All Human Life* exhibition and this handsome pictorial souvenir.

The scale of the selection effort has been extraordinary. Bruce Bernard, our selector, and Sue Percival who has assisted him at Hulton Deutsch have had to rummage through hundreds of thousands of prints in the hope of bringing some cohesiveness to a selection of under five hundred prints that would represent the best of the collection. Many other selections could be made out of such a sizeable archive that would be entirely different and bear no comparison to this present one. But we are sure that the one arrived at for this show contains insights and sentiments that have a relevance to our existence today, and fully justifies the title we have chosen.

Our thanks go to Bruce Bernard for bearing the burden of selection in his inimitable way and to Sue Percival whose knowledge of the collection has been invaluable to this process, and who, along with Brigitte Lardinois and Jane Alison at Barbican Art Gallery, has resolutely steered the project through to fruition. Thanks also to Matthew Butson and Harriet Orr for their help with the multi-media installations, to Marguerite Zaubermann for her enthusiasm and backup, and all in the darkroom and conservation studio for ensuring the highest quality of exhibition prints.

Finally, our heartfelt thanks go to our sponsors, especially Apple Computer U.K. Limited for the loan of equipment for the CD-Rom display, and Reuters for the provision of their News Pictures Service. Without their support it would not have been possible to realise the exhibition so successfully.

Brian Deutsch
Managing Director
Hulton Deutsch Collection

John Hoole
Curator
Barbican Art Gallery

The Hulton Deutsch Collection

Sue Percival

There is nothing like selecting an exhibition to make you realise the enormity of the Hulton Deutsch Collection. Myriad possibilities for exhibitions lurk in the hundreds of boxes and row upon row of filing cabinets and shelves, full of not only photographs but books and engravings too. All of it amassed to service the Hulton publishing empire, and in particular the one publication for which it is famous above all else, *Picture Post*. People might not be familiar with 'the Hulton' but will have heard of *Picture Post*, as it still has a place in the hearts of many people and has had a lasting influence on many more. In the introduction to his book *Photodiscovery* Bruce Bernard recalls the impact of seeing in one issue Howlett's memorable portrait of Isambard Kingdom Brunel standing in front of the enormous launching chains of the steamship Great Eastern, an image not immediately associated with *Picture Post*, or indeed the Hulton Deutsch Collection. Images such as this one from the earliest days of photography would appear regularly in issues of Britain's favourite weekly and so form an important part of the library. Now, nearly forty years since *Picture Post* folded, it is not mere nostalgia to turn its pages. The quality of many of the features, both in terms of the photographs and the written word, means that it retains its freshness and many of the issues it tackled have relevance today.

It is impossible to talk about the Hulton Deutsch Collection without mentioning *Picture Post*, but there are many other collections which play a significant part in *All Human Life*. This exhibition is about everyday human experience, the mundane but not the dull. Many of the best photographs are not taken by the 'greats' of photography.

Indeed it is often the subject matter which shines through, eclipsing all thoughts of the maker. With now forgotten press agencies like Topical Press and Fox Photos, the photographer was never credited, and although they remain anonymous today they have produced some of our strongest images. It was only in 1944, six years after it first appeared, that *Picture Post* photographers themselves got a credit in the magazine and the likes of Kurt Hutton and Bert Hardy became known to the public they were entertaining. And although there is now a separate archive within the collection where the work of Bill Brandt or Kertész can be viewed, it is a new development – not long ago their photographs were treated the same as any others, as working prints filed away according to their subject matter and therefore scattered across the collection.

Bruce Bernard and I have worked our way through the files and boxes, dipping in and out of subjects a shelf at a time. Choosing which subject to delve into each day was no problem; subconsciously I would find myself immersed in whatever news story had cast its spell the night before. After the Grand National fiasco it was 'Sport: Horseracing' that I looked at, and all the talk of the close of Swan Hunters shipyard on the Tyne had me engrossed in the 'Sea: Dock (Bri): Newcastle' section. The Keystone Agency archive, comprising some three million images – in terms of Hulton Deutsch collections a fairly recent acquisition – proved to be a constant source of fascinating material: where else could you find a whole box of images on telegraph poles or topiary!

I am not sure how many of the fifteen million images at the Hulton we have looked at over the the past year. Each file on any one subject is full of photographs from many different collections. Of course, in every file there are duds and duplicates, but there is always the expectation of finding that one image which stands out – the one you want to look at time and time again. There have been favourites along the way, many of them joint ones and we always knew which were the ones we each would reject.

Amongst my own personal favourites are pictures of some of the old characters who you might still, if you are fortunate enough, stumble across every now and again in the course of daily life. They may only illuminate your day for a few seconds, but here there is time to linger over them – people like old Tom Owen, the hedge-laying specialist, loving every moment of his hair cut in the fantastical shed of the village postman-cum-cobbler-cum-barber, Handel Lewis.

All Human Life perfectly describes the selection of images in the exhibition and with it the strength of the Hulton Deutsch Collection. The illustrious historian Charles Gibbs-Smith who had the job of setting up a system of classification for the library in the 1940s described how the Directors of the Hulton Press wanted to 'set up a library of illustrations covering every "picturable" subject and activity on earth.' The subjects and activities in this exhibition form the common thread that link us all. This is not the history of photography or the story of photo-journalism but a window onto a precious life that may all too easily be taken for granted.

I love to watch peoples' faces as they enter the cavernous interior of the Hulton Deutsch building for the first time, the facade of which is very unpromising. On the day I arrived for my interview nearly four years ago, I remember walking down the grimy cobbled street in West London in the pouring rain, standing outside and thinking 'so this is the worlds biggest photo-library!' But in common with all visitors, you are given a tour, and when you first see the size of the warehouses, one storing photographs and the other negatives, you get a shock – they are huge! I went away on that dreary winter day full of excitement, an excitement I am pleased to say has not diminished; if anything it has grown, especially working throughout 1993 on *All Human Life*.

All Human Life

Bruce Bernard

This book is intended as an enjoyable souvenir for those who have seen the exhibition *All Human Life*, as well as an equally enjoyable look at photography from an unfamiliar angle for those who were unable to get there. There have been exhibitions of photographs taken for newspapers and magazines in the past, but they have never shown so many pictures from quite so many sources or kinds of publication. Neither have any of them given the viewer a chance to compare them on the spot with some high quality work unrelated to journalism of any kind. The title chosen for the exhibition seemed the most appropriate one, as the voracious camera has pursued and been paid to pursue every kind of human being in every kind of situation and extremity – from good fortune and happiness to disaster and misery, as well as assiduously recording human vanity of both the relatively harmless and the deadliest kinds. It has of course lied, half-lied and overlooked the truth, quite apart from being deliberately used for all kinds of deception and propaganda. If Nazism was in part a triumph of graphic design in the service of evil, then it was the camera which most widely and often enthusiastically distributed its deadly poison. Happily photography has also done sterling service on behalf of humanity, so it is evidently as much a power for good and evil as the written or spoken word.

Most pictures in newspapers and magazines are experienced with a variety of feelings according to their subject matter and power as images – and then forgotten. Great or sensational ones are remembered, and occasionally reproduced again, or even again and again until they become part of our imaginative stock. Others, often equally interesting and sometimes more beautiful, fade beyond recall and need to be revived in books or exhibitions such as this one, where they can provide fresh enjoyment, enlightenment or cause for reflection.

No one person is ever likely to see every single image in the Hulton Deutsch Collection, as there are about 15,000,000 of them. So the exhibition has had to be selected from the 200,000 or so prints that I, with some very welcome and intelligent assistance from Sue Percival, the Curator of the Collection, was able to look at over nine months. Having been guided to the most promising areas though, I think I may actually have seen half of the best pictures, though I will never know how many masterpieces I have missed.

The pictures were chosen with no rigid preconceptions. After a reconnaissance of about a month I realised that the exhibition must be mainly about the wide variety of human beings they cover, hence the exhibition's title. The photographs that were finally selected were the ones which could, in a sense, transcend their original function and survive the test of hanging on a wall and the consequent repeated inspection.

With a few notable exceptions, the pictures in *All Human Life* were taken specifically for use in popular magazines by professionals, many of whom, it seems likely, would have had little interest in photography as an art, some perhaps even feeling superior to that kind of thing.

The medium had to wait over forty years, after Talbot and Daguerre produced the first satisfactory and permanent images, for the introduction of the half-tone screen and block and its consequent reproduction in newspapers and magazines. But photography had already been used as a basis for engraved illustrations and was therefore well prepared for its greatly extended function. There were excellent magazines, such as *The Sphere*, which in due course used it well, but newspapers were slower and the quality papers disdained to use it for some time. The popular picture magazines we know or knew as vehicles for high quality photographs, originated in Europe during the Twenties. *Picture Post* was conceived in 1937 by a genius from Hungary, Stefan Lorant, who had already edited the British magazine *Illustrated* and invented the brilliant pocket magazine *Lilliput* with its famously entertaining photographic juxtapositions and puns.

There is no doubt that the soul of the exhibition resides in the pictures taken for *Picture Post*, whether they were actually reproduced in it or not. There never was a popular magazine quite so sensitively concerned with the lives and problems of ordinary people or so committed to the idea of ordinary human decency in something like the sense that George Orwell used the words. Its photographers, among them a refugee from Nazi Germany, Kurt Hutton (Kurt Hübschmann), seemed inspired by the opportunities it offered them, and our own Bert Hardy's robust amiability combined with his first class talent helped to make the magazine a truly thought provoking and heart warming fourpenny-worth. This book demonstrates how excellent they and many of the other lensmen could be. John Chillingworth and Charles Hewitt, for instance, are now much more than names to me.

The second richest and to me the most surprising source of images has been the Topical Press agency collection. The 35 mm Leica was not used by journalists when most of the agency's best pictures were taken and the larger format 5 × 4 inch negatives produced some wonderfully sharp images and insights into everday life of the 1910s, '20s and '30s. Sometimes we framed their contact prints which possess a magic that is difficult to define.

We decided to show a large number of images from all sources as 'vintage' prints (those made soon after taking the picture), even when the original negative still exists (though sometimes from necessity because it doesn't). They often convey a more resonant sense of reality, partly because they are never pure black and white, something which photographers never sought in any case, and which was first dictated by printers' ink and newsprint, even if the latter could never quite attain purest white. Neither are modern photographic papers the same as those used half a century or more ago, and they can threaten a once living image with something equivalent to rigor mortis.

Also the gradual yellowing or any other alteration in the colour of old prints quite often seems to grant them a life of their own. No photographer or printer chose these tints, so they can tell us something of their successful struggle with time and decay and make us welcome their survival as partly self-made images in which both colour and tonality often seem more beautiful or appropriate than in a modern print.

It is evident that the best work of artist photographers is more concerned with ideas and is in general more formally beautiful than any magazine or newspaper picture, but sometimes a quite anonymous journeyman has preserved a moment of life as miraculously, or because of his lowly status, perhaps more so, than the likes of Edward Steichen or Julia Margaret Cameron. It matters not that the photograph of the two little girls with a sack of coal on their pushchair reproduced in this selection is not particularly well composed. The photographer has captured the actual in a way that makes it seem for a moment that life itself has been preserved. No doubt interest could not be sustained in it for as long or as deeply as with the work of the great photographers, (it might even get rather irritating). But none of them could surely have performed such a bright little miracle with the everyday.

The enlivening quality of such a photograph seems to actually lie in a lack of firm preconception or concern with the whole picture on the part of the photographer, and the pleasure it offers seems wonderfully pure, rather like a surprise encounter with a good friend thought to be far away.

There are several pictures here which I hope will raise a smile if not a laugh. But there is a kind of cutely composed photograph that can provoke amused interest for a split second and then dies forever. They sometimes make popular postcards but too often have a shallow glibness or vacuity that I devoutly wish photography was unable to convey. But there is also a kind of silly photograph that can remain permanently amusing. In this book, although it mocks its subject, I particularly liked the one of the singing cooper, and another of the dog opening the gate in a huge circus arena, watched it seems by hundreds of people – an absurd but rather touching scene.

In this book, Derek Birdsall, its designer, has made juxtapositions of images rather in the spirit of the early years of *Lilliput* magazine. This provides a pleasure which I think does not demean or trivialise the subject matter – the occasional comic relief sometimes afforded even helping one to return to the serious import of serious pictures refreshed by this brief indulgence. The exhibition is in any case as much about the human comedy as about human suffering or endurance, and it would be intolerable if photography did not allow us to distance ourselves from its subject matter, even when entirely pleasant. I hope that this book, and the exhibition from which it is derived provide, as well as harmless pleasure, a sense of the power of the photograph to foster mutual human understanding – sometimes unhappily through its conveyance of awkward home truths, the prevalence of inhumanity, and the absurdity of human pretensions and behaviour. But also in its ability to make us like people whom we can never meet or would never have been likely to. The photograph can certainly broaden our imaginative horizons, and it can also deepen our understanding of those whom its evidence suggests are as important a part of human life as we are.

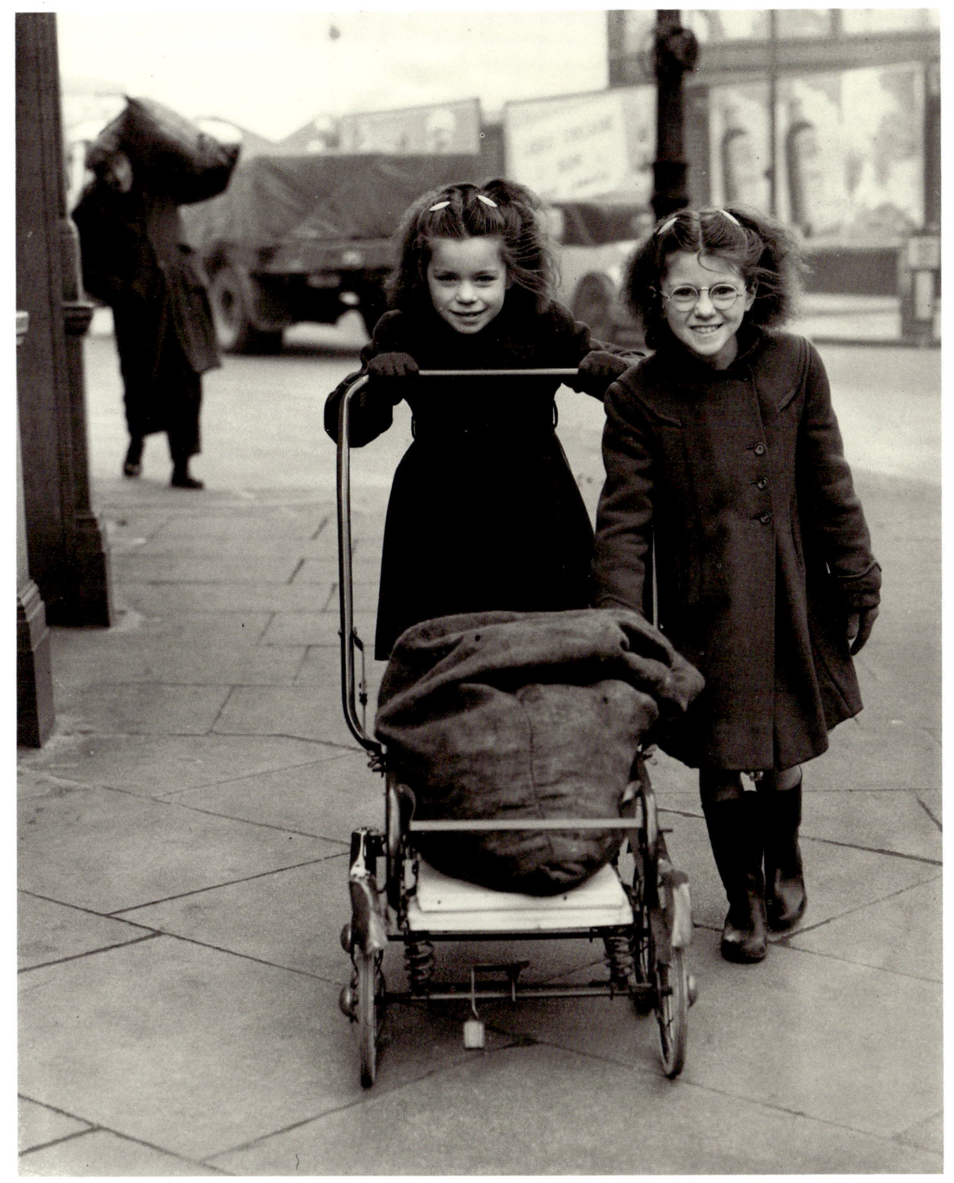

Photographer unknown, Fox photos
Bringing Home the Coke, *12 March 1955*

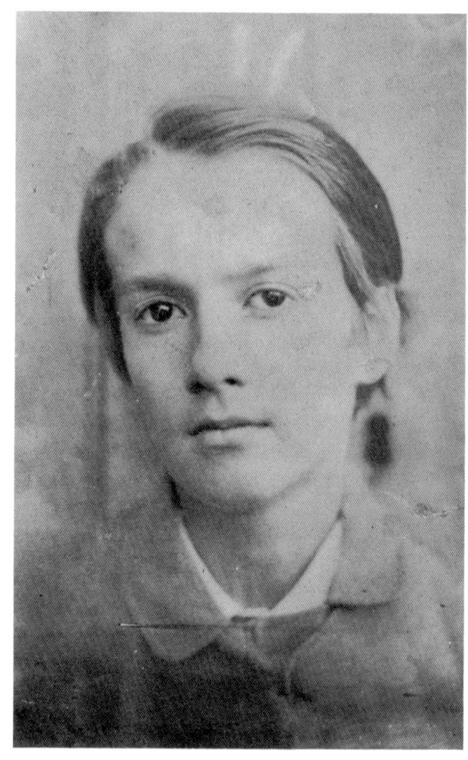

Attributed to O.G. Rejlander
William Bayley, Julia Margaret Cameron's nephew, *1858*

Julia Margaret Cameron
Charles Hay Cameron, *c1866–70*

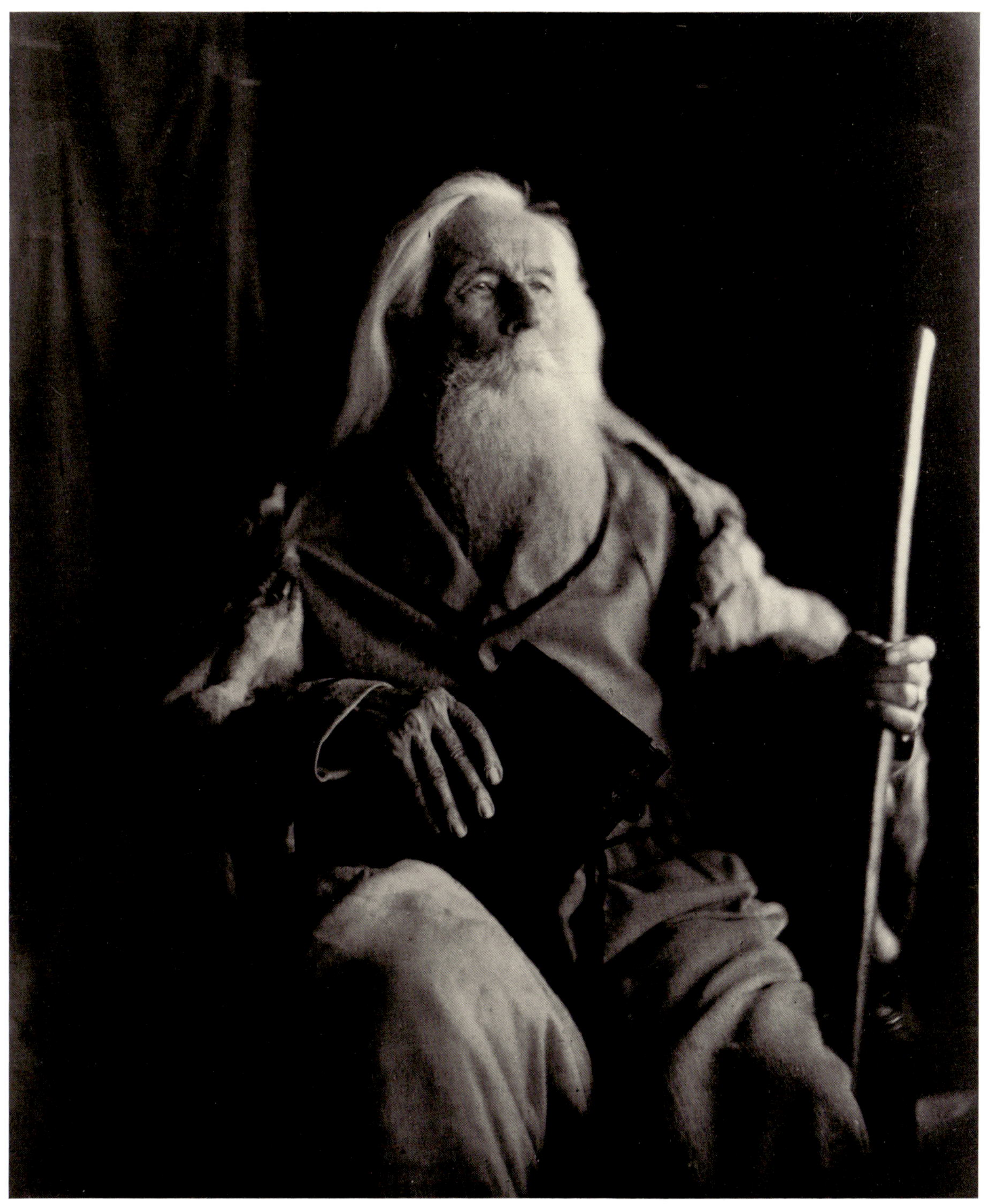

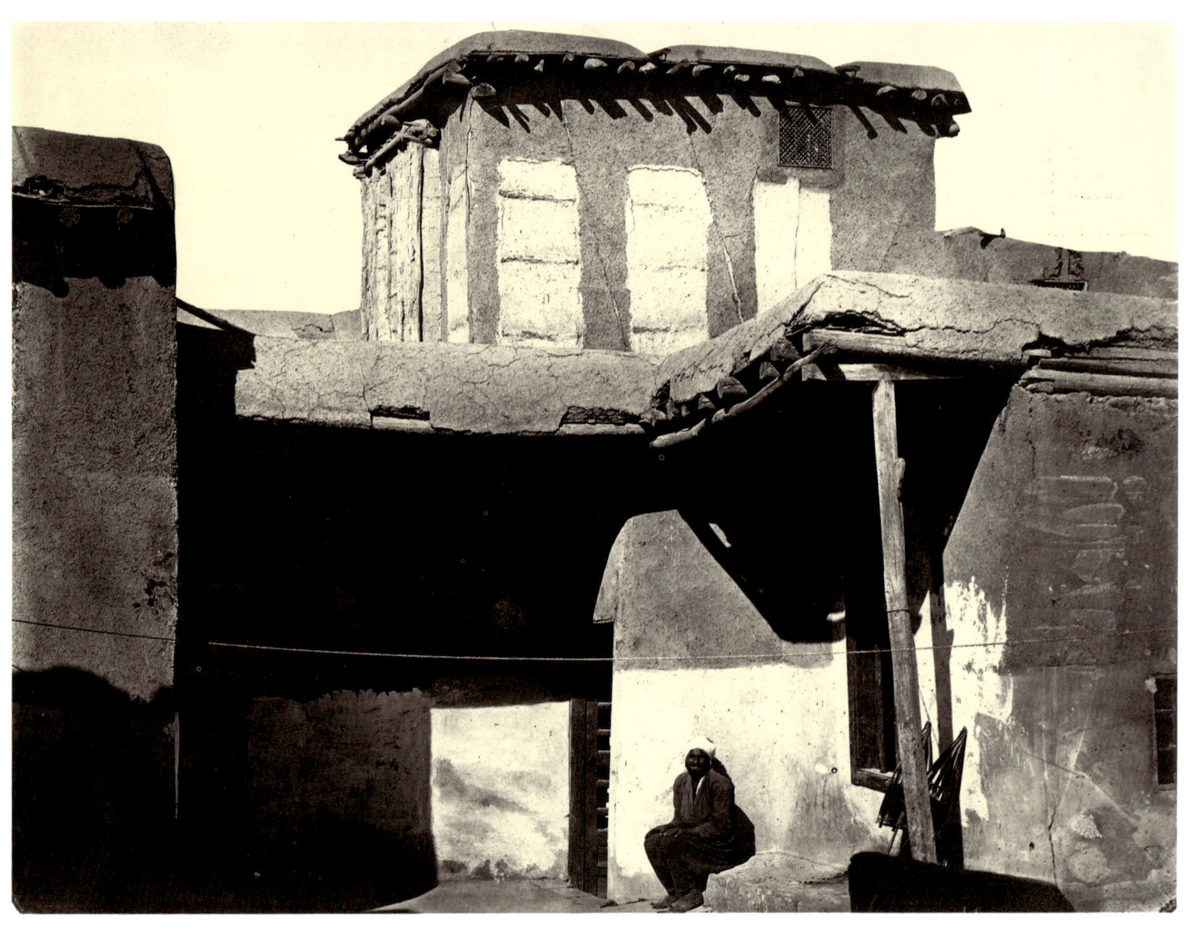

Felix Bonfils
House of Ananias, Damascus, *c1870*

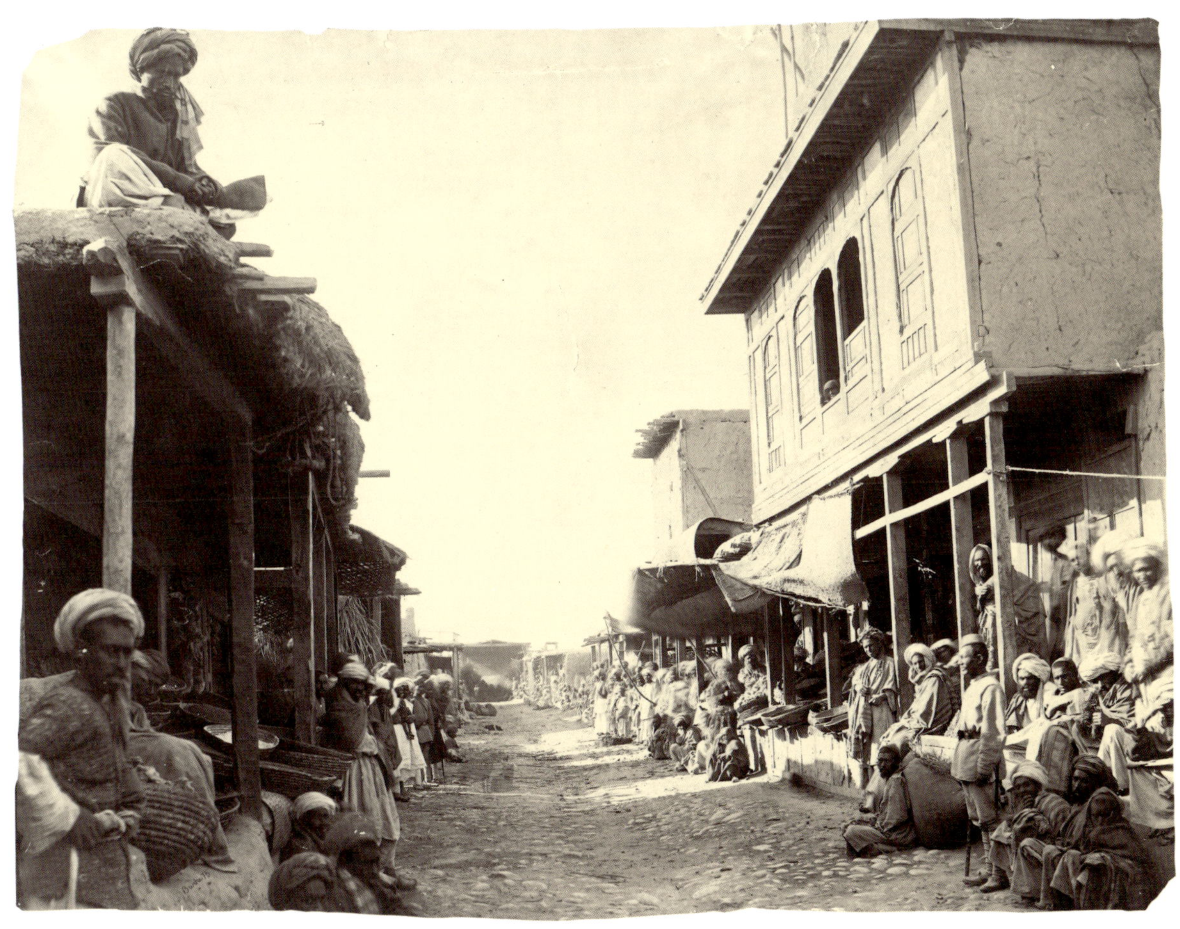

James Burke
Street in Jalalabad, Afghanistan, *c1880*

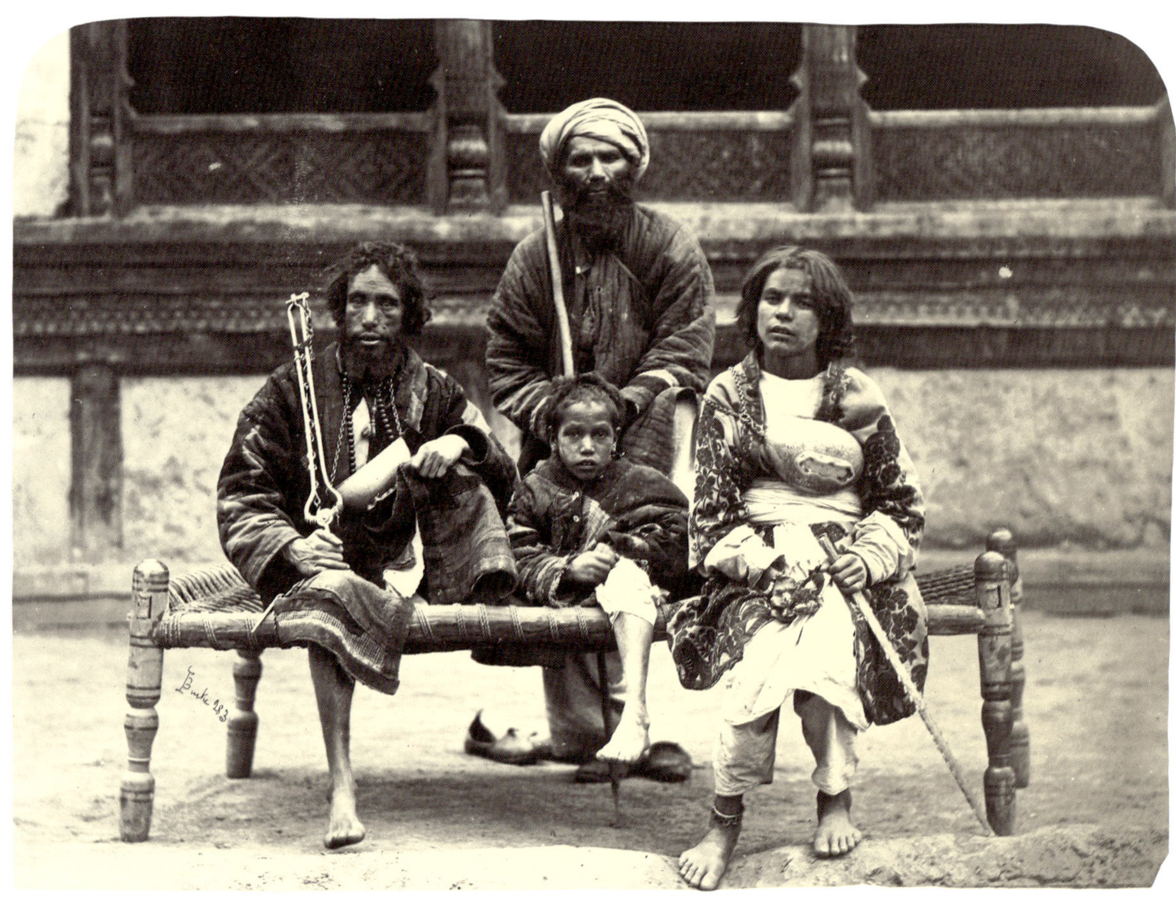

James Burke
'Group of characteristic beggars', Afghanistan, *c1880*

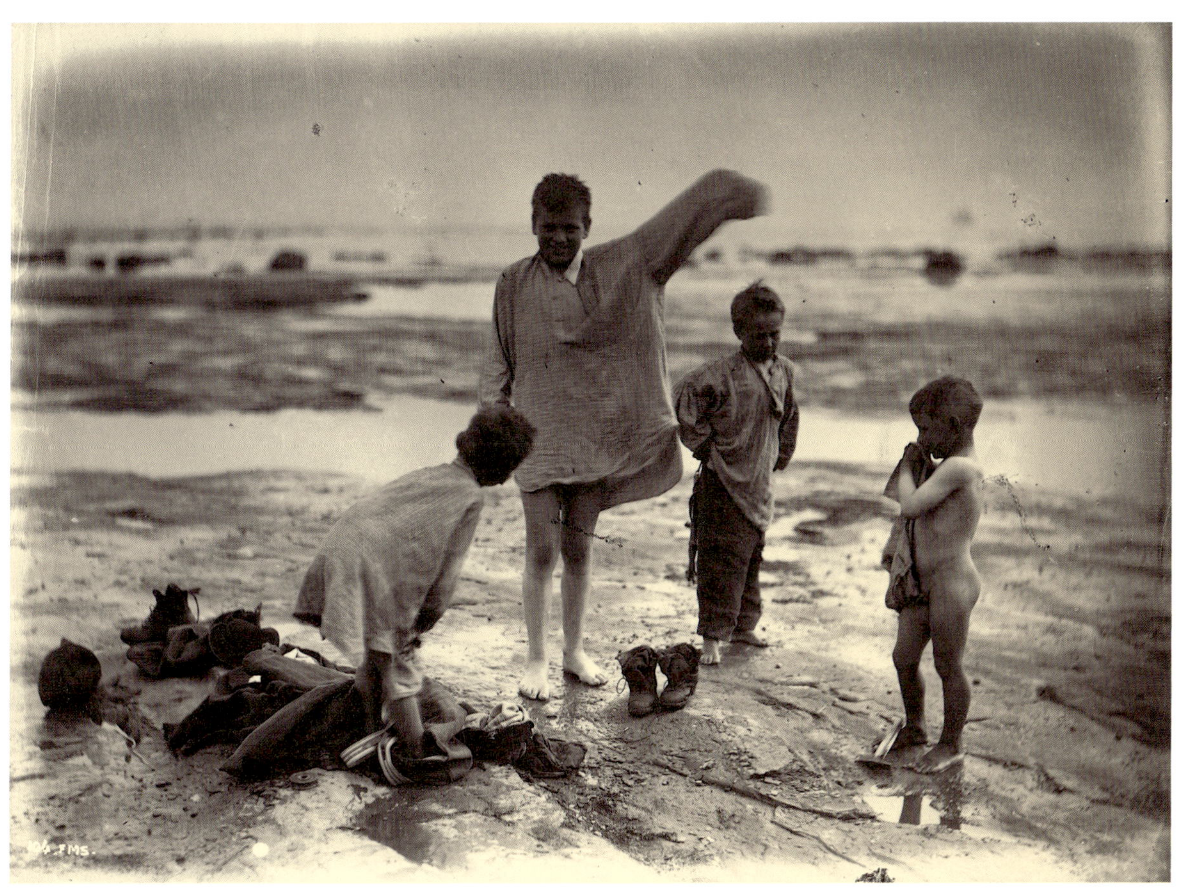

Frank Meadow Sutcliffe
Boys on Beach, Whitby, *1880s*

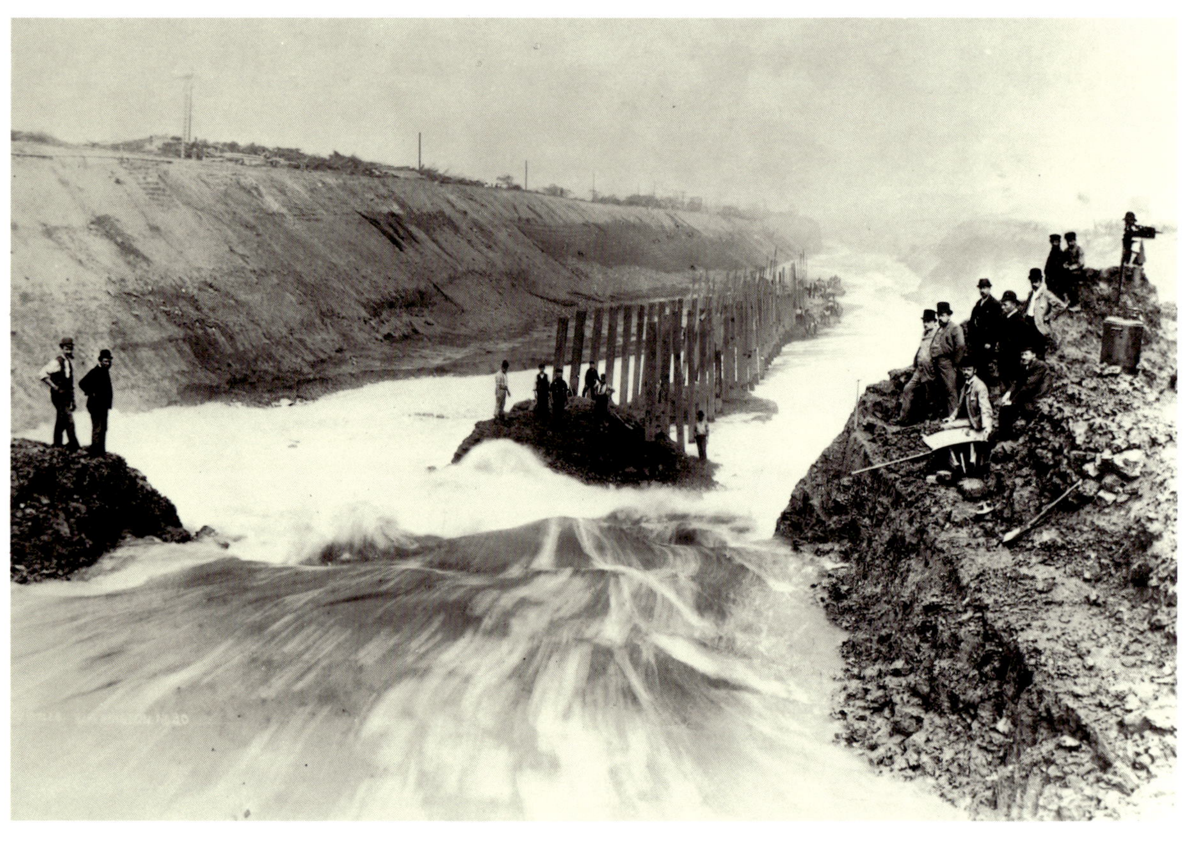

Birtles of Warrington
Construction of the Manchester Ship Canal, *1894*
Letting in the water at Ellesmere Port with E. L. Williams and
other engineers.

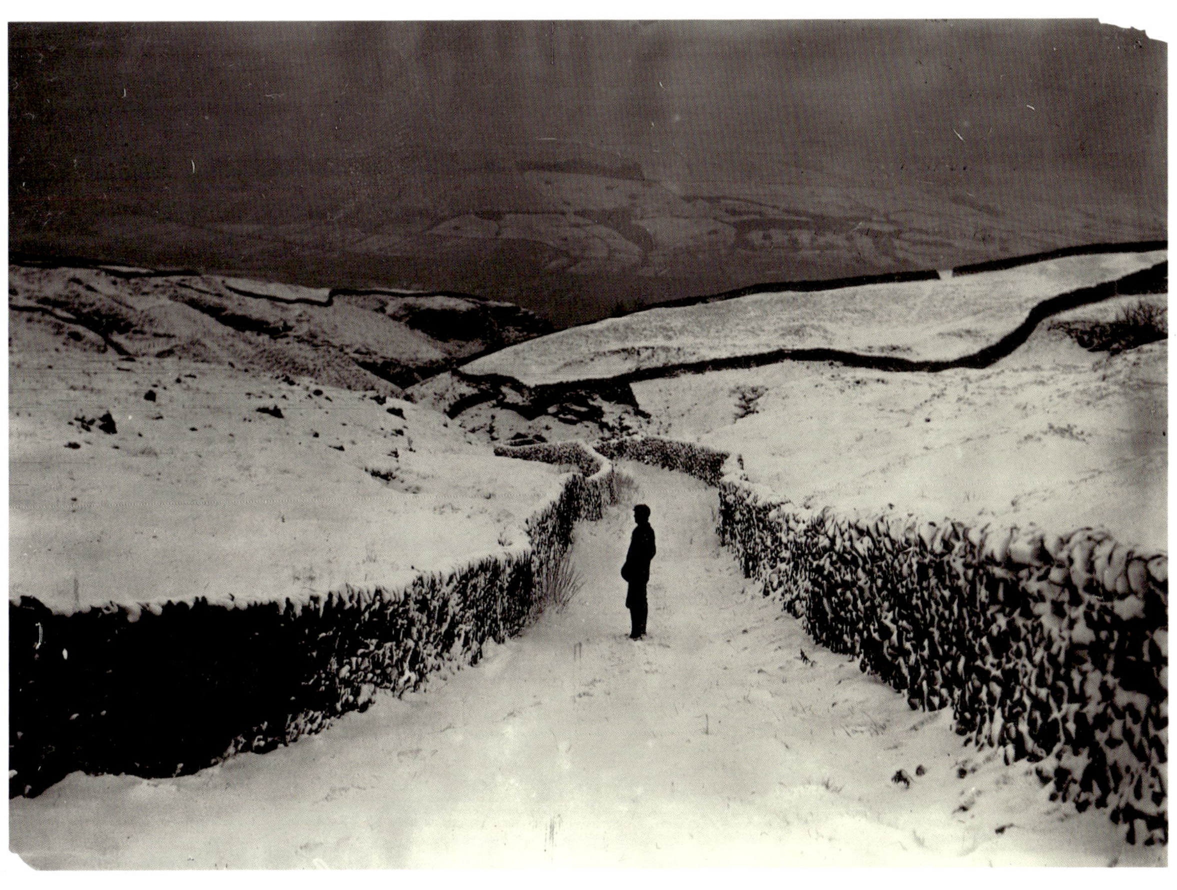

Photographer unknown, Topical Press
Fluor Spar – lead picking in the snow, *December 1909*

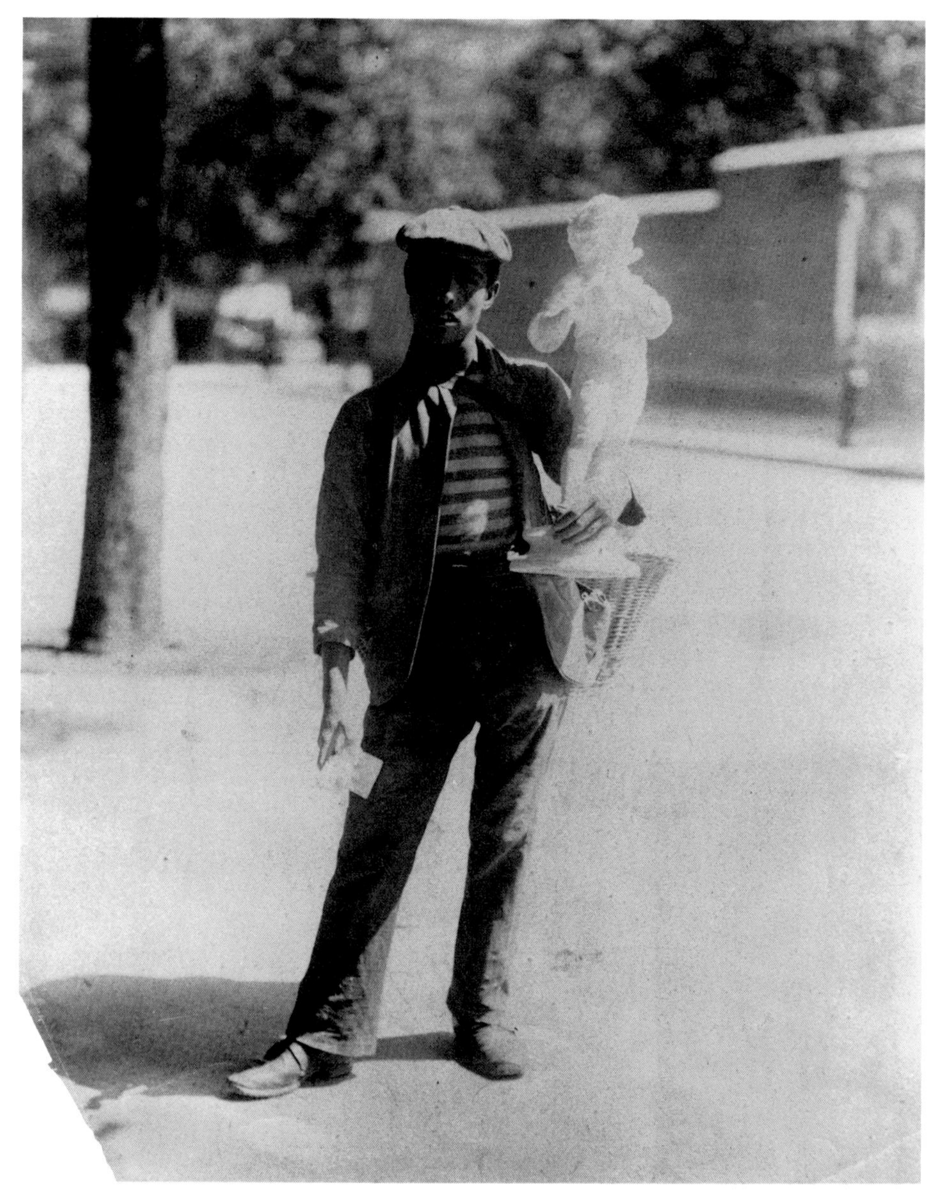

Photographer unknown
Boy selling statuettes, Paris, *c1900*

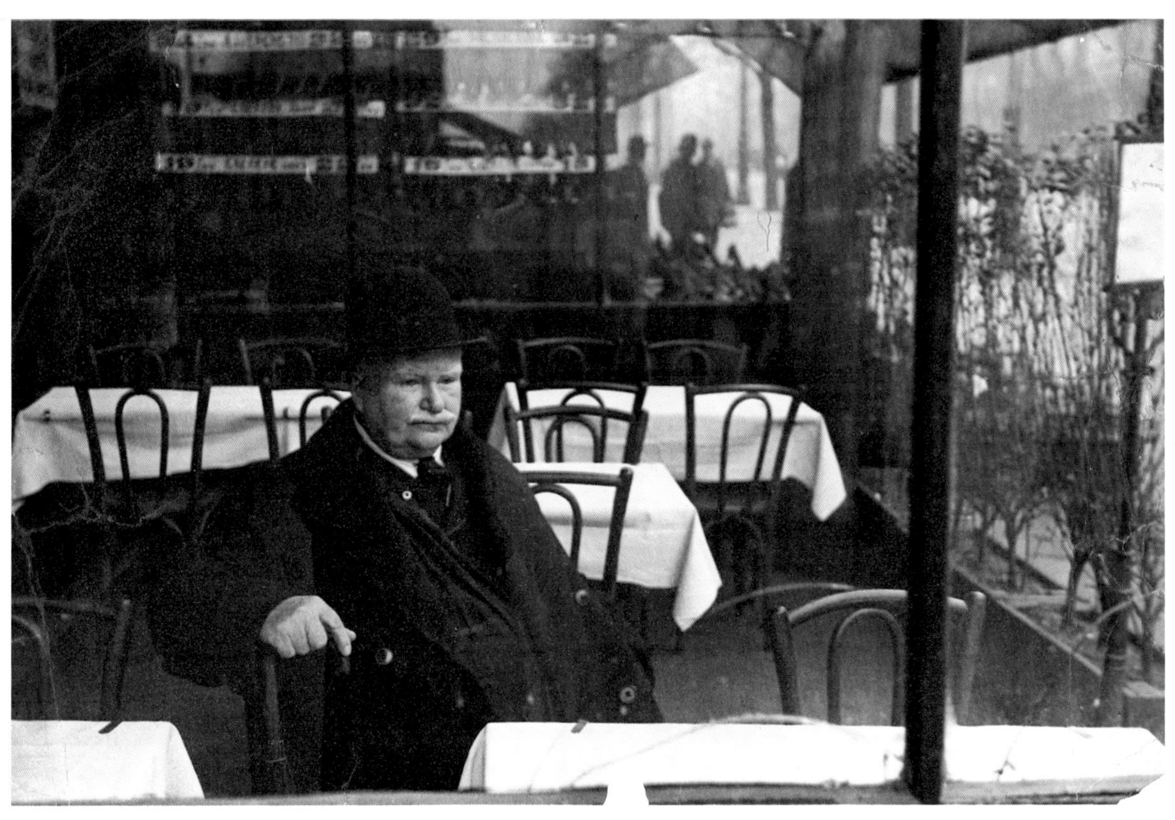

Henri-Cartier Bresson
An old gentleman seated on the glazed terrace of a café near Montparnasse station, *1934*

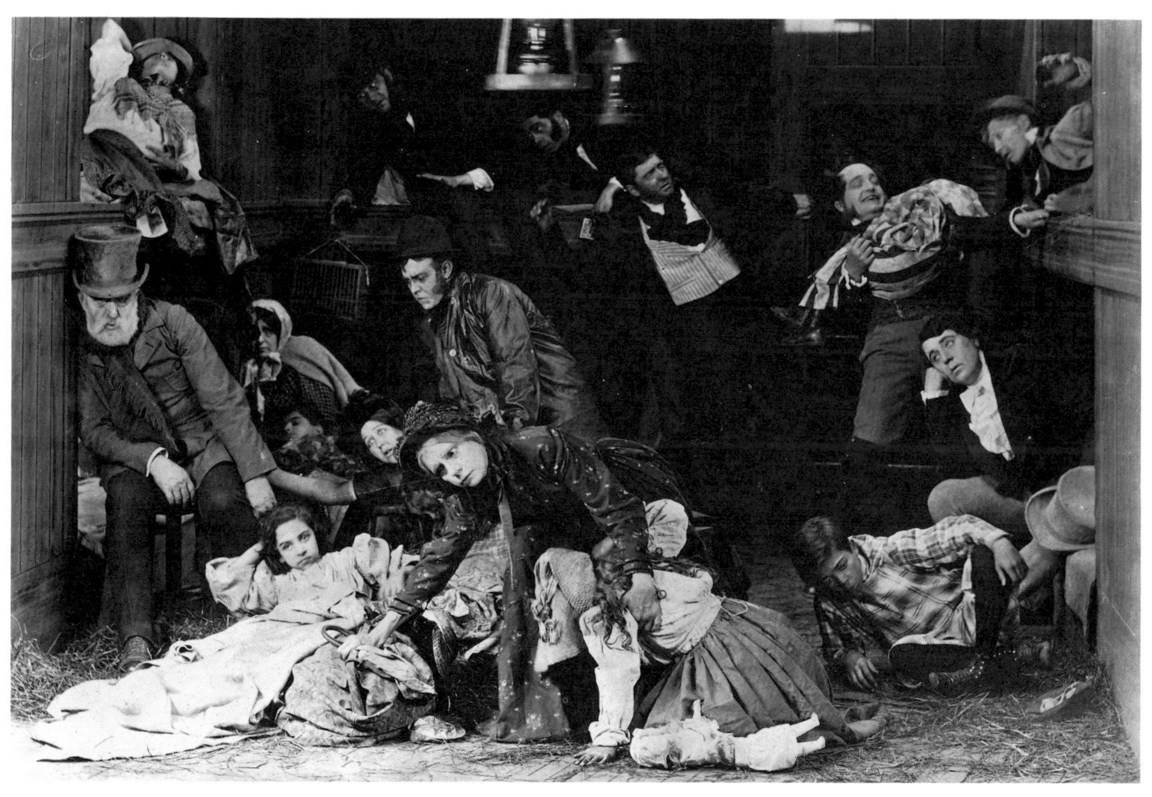

Photographer unknown, Daily Mirror Library
Ship scene from 'Martin Chuzzlewitt' – in the steerage on the way to America, *February 1912*

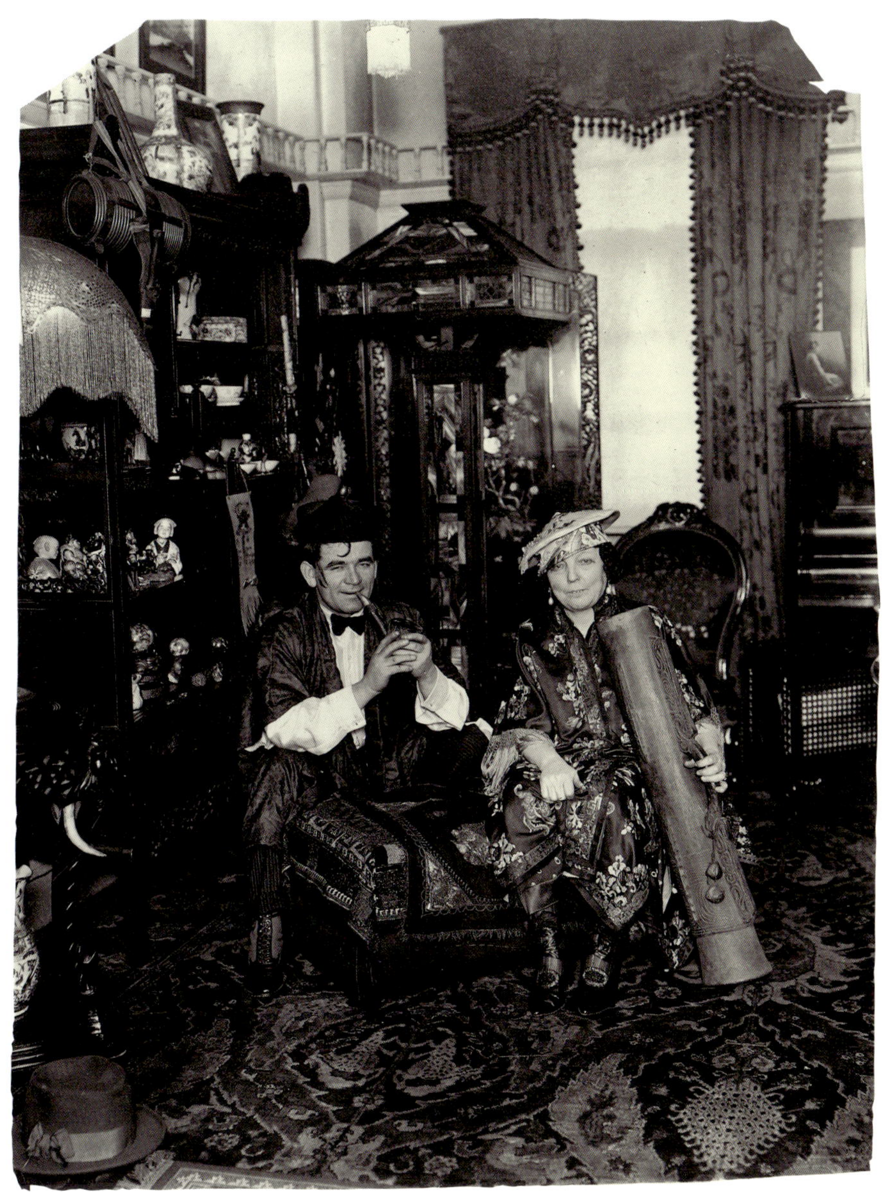

Photographer unknown, Topical Press

Miss Marie Lloyd with her husband Bernard Dillon at their home in Golders Green, *c1920*

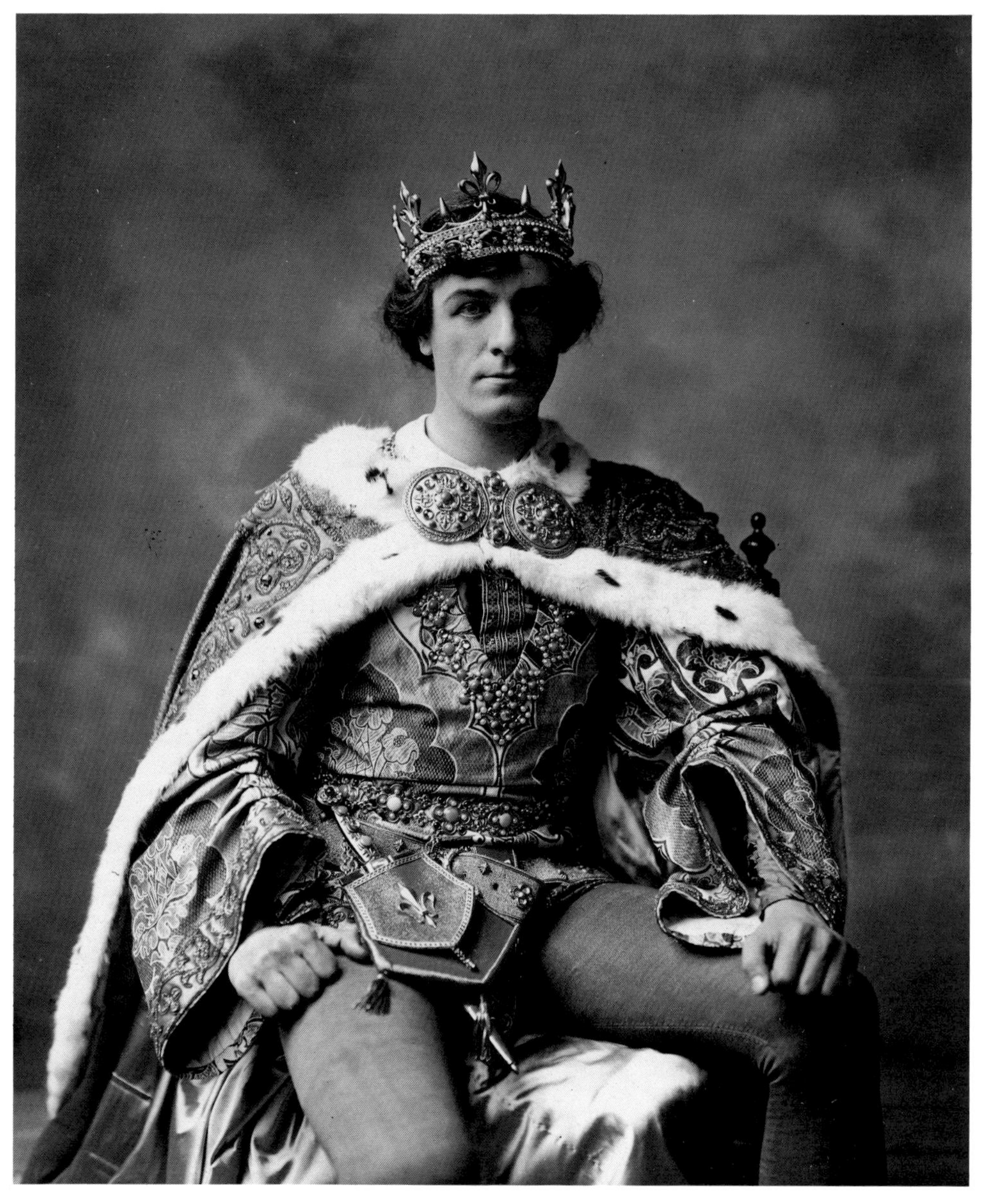

Photographer unknown, Daily Mirror Library
**Mr. Matheson Lang as 'King Robert of Sicily' in the production of
'The Proud Prince' at the Lyceum**, *1909*

Cecil Beaton
Vivien Leigh in a scene from 'Caesar and Cleopatra', *1945*

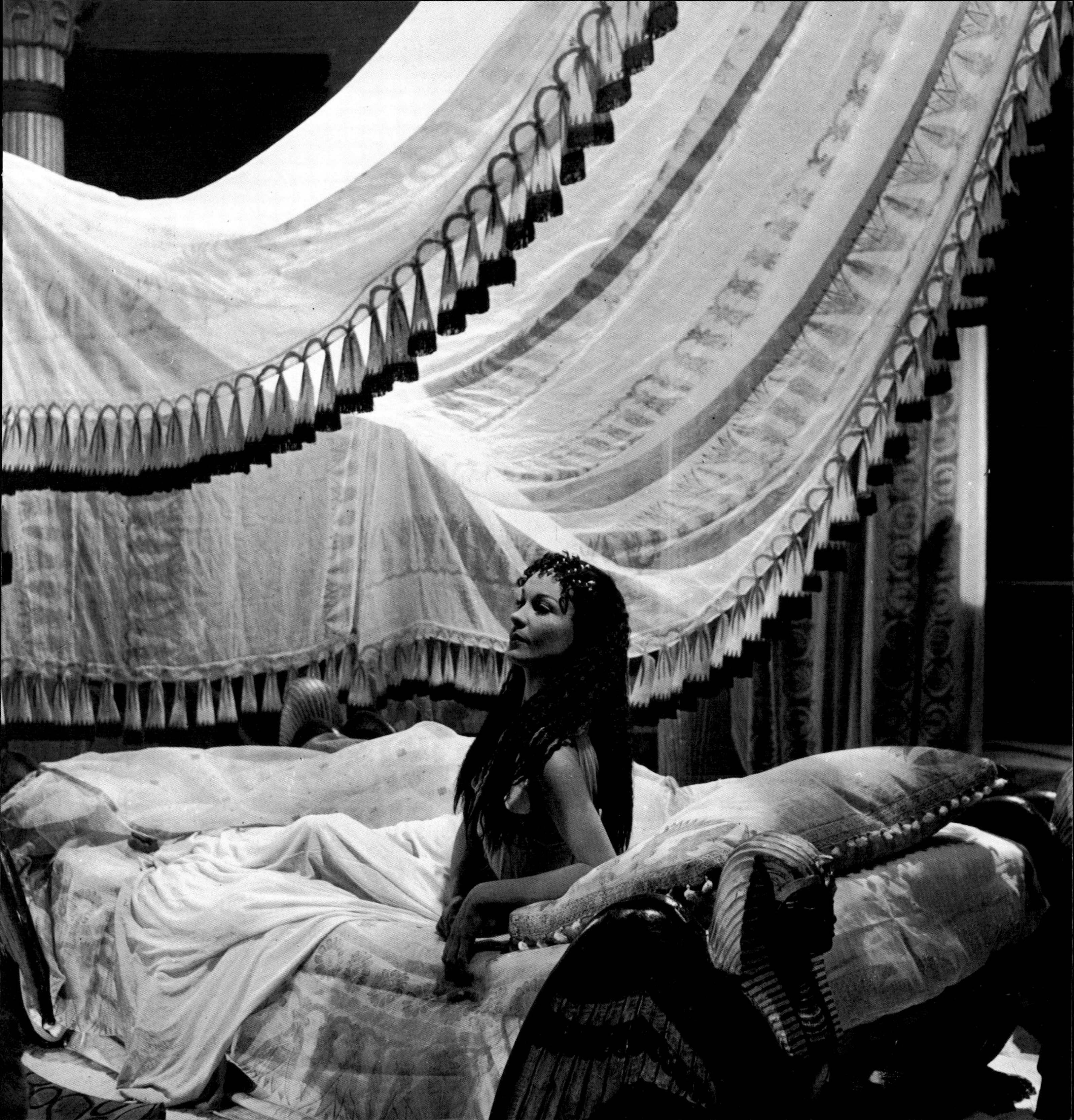

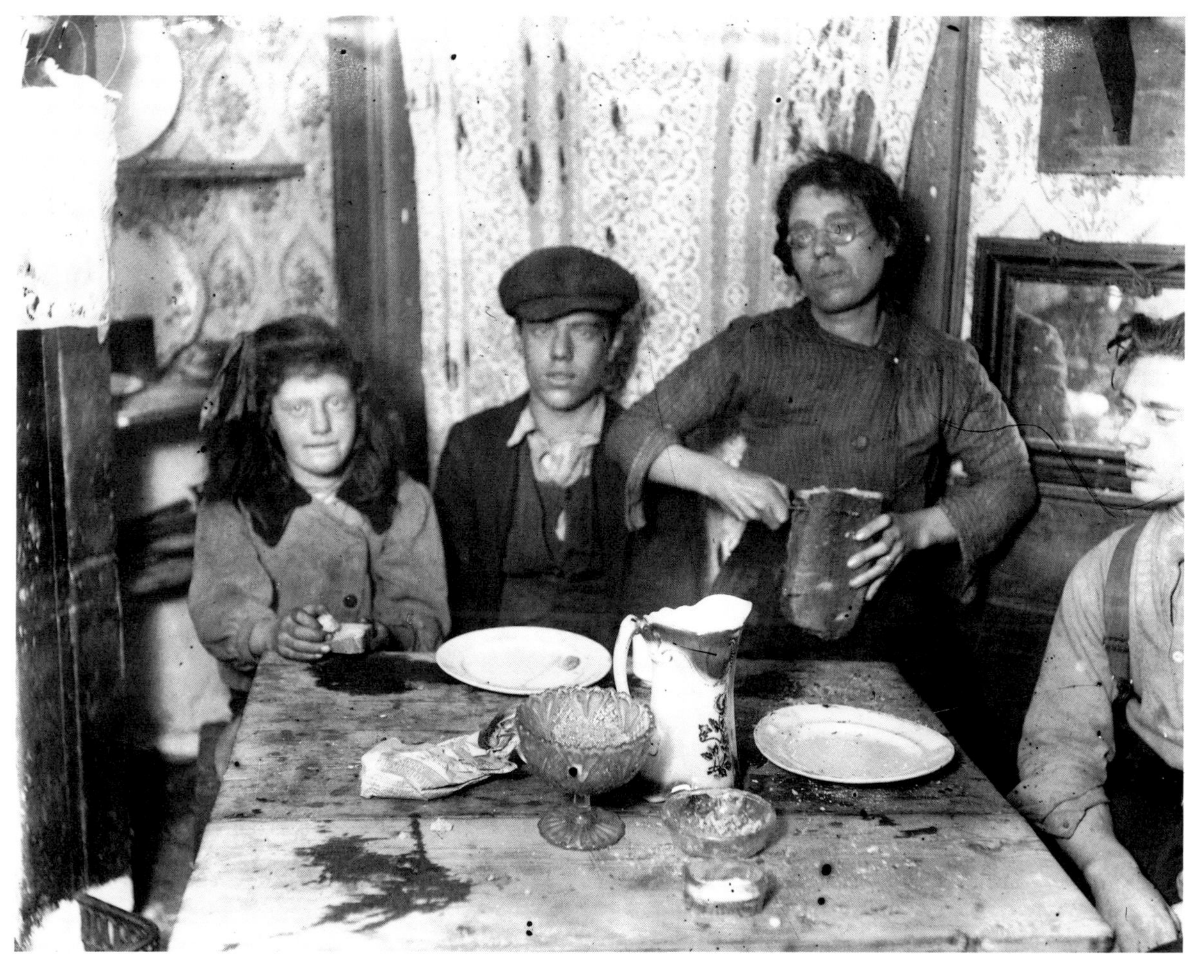

Photographer unknown, Topical Press
Slums at Shadwell, *December 1920*

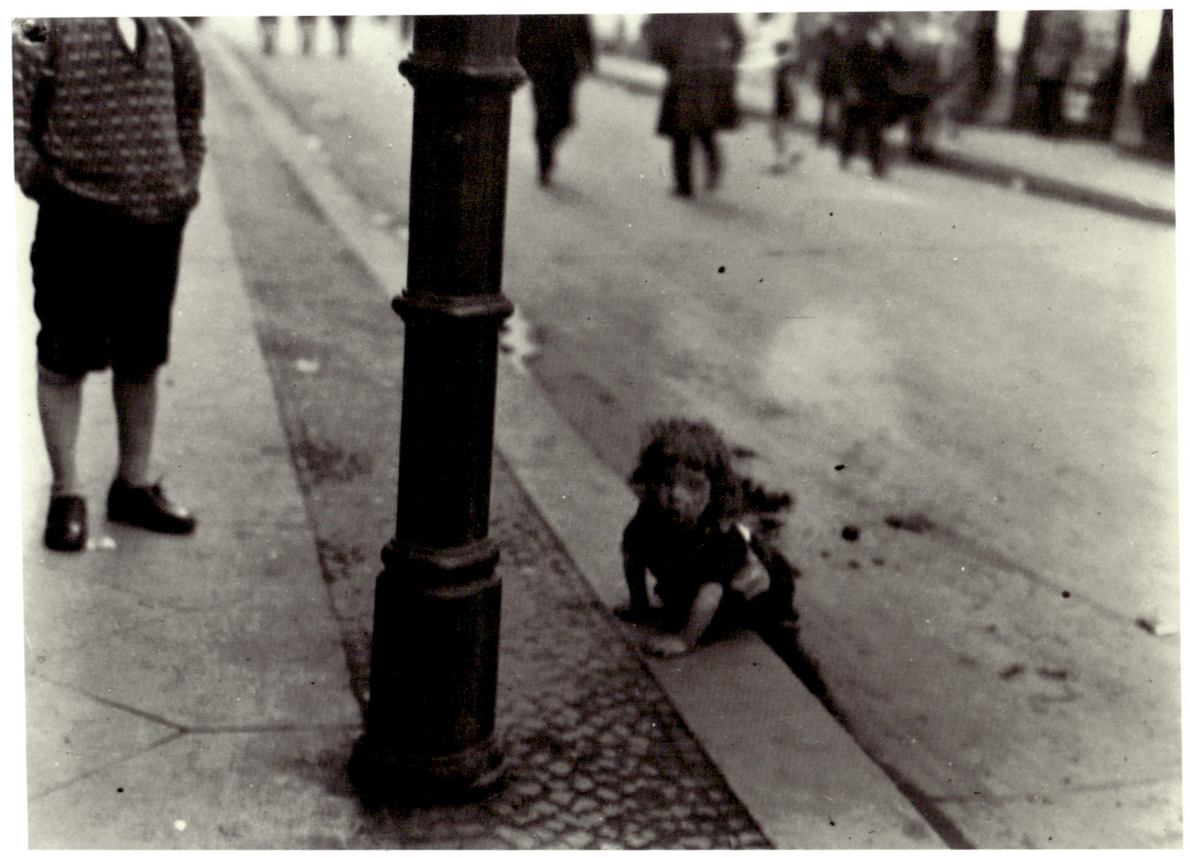

Photographer unknown, Ecce Photo
Untitled, *c1920 (Berlin)*

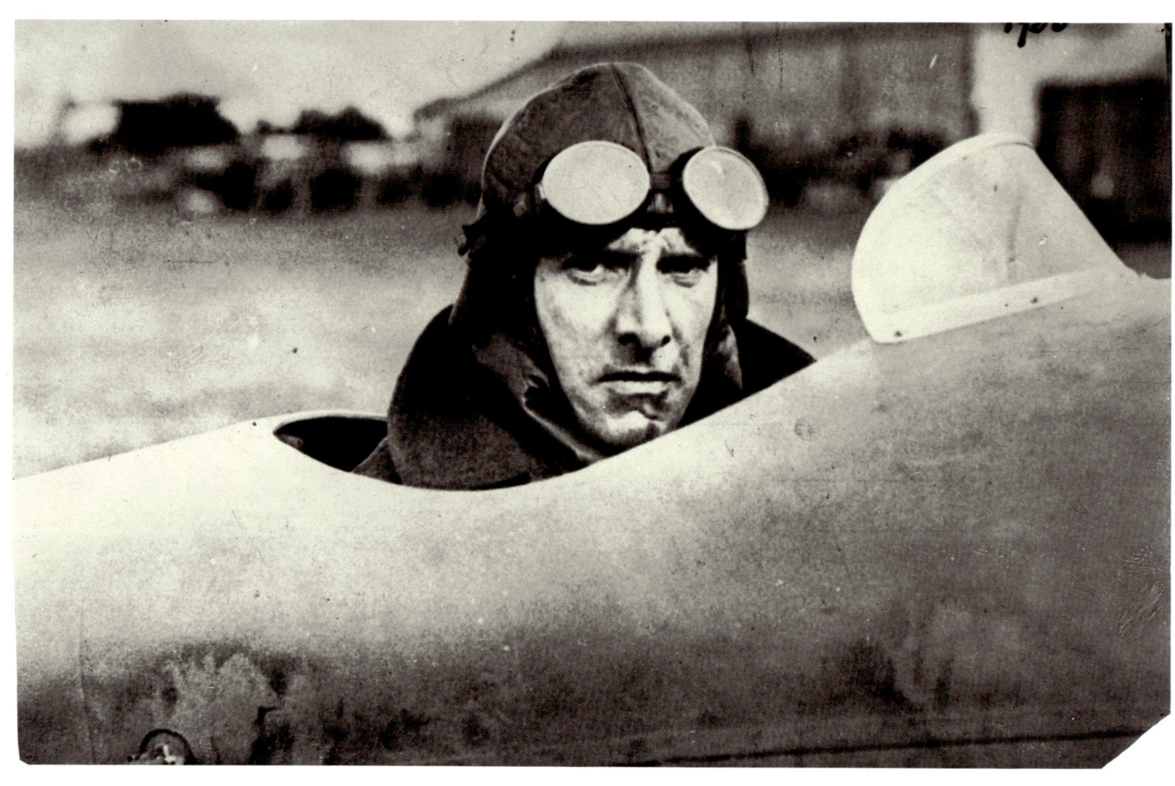

Photographer unknown
Sir Geoffrey de Havilland, British Aircraft Designer, *(undated)*

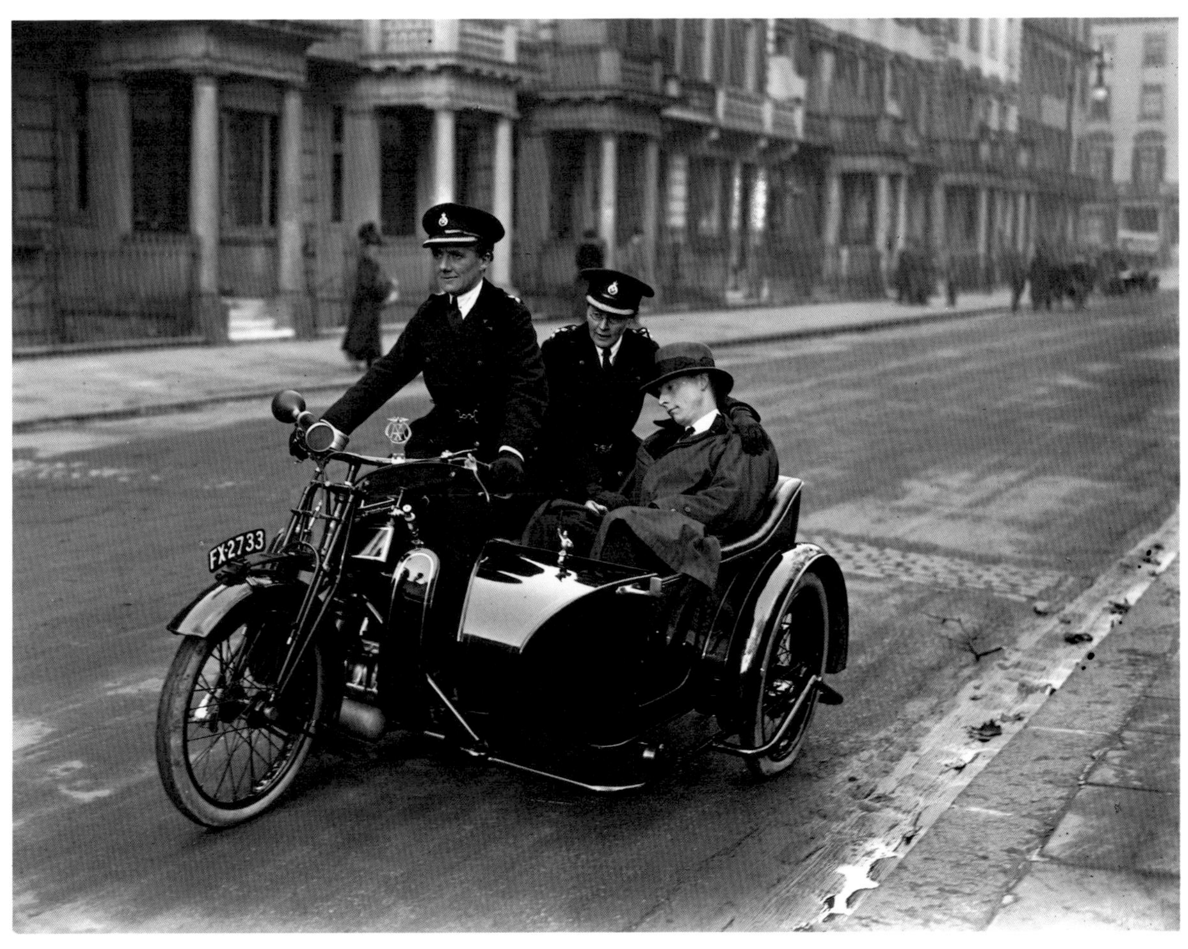

Photographer unknown, Topical Press
The Motor Women Police, 'how to deal with a drunken man',
January 1920

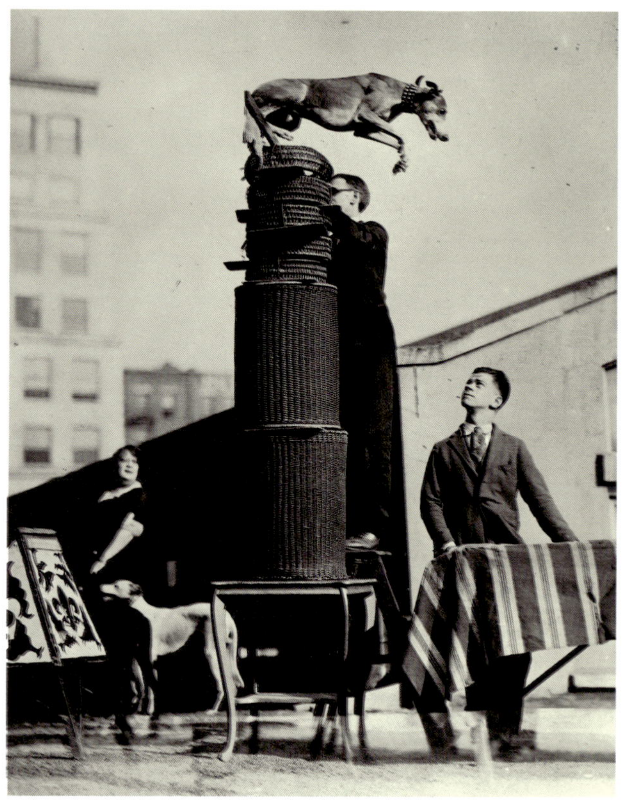

Photographer unknown, Topical Press
Rambling Gold, Champion Dog Jumper, *2 December 1925*

Photographer unknown, Keystone
Piano and Player, *undated*
'Alexander Marshall takes the strain on his shoulders and abdomen as a piano and player is rested on a yoke on his knees and shoulders.'

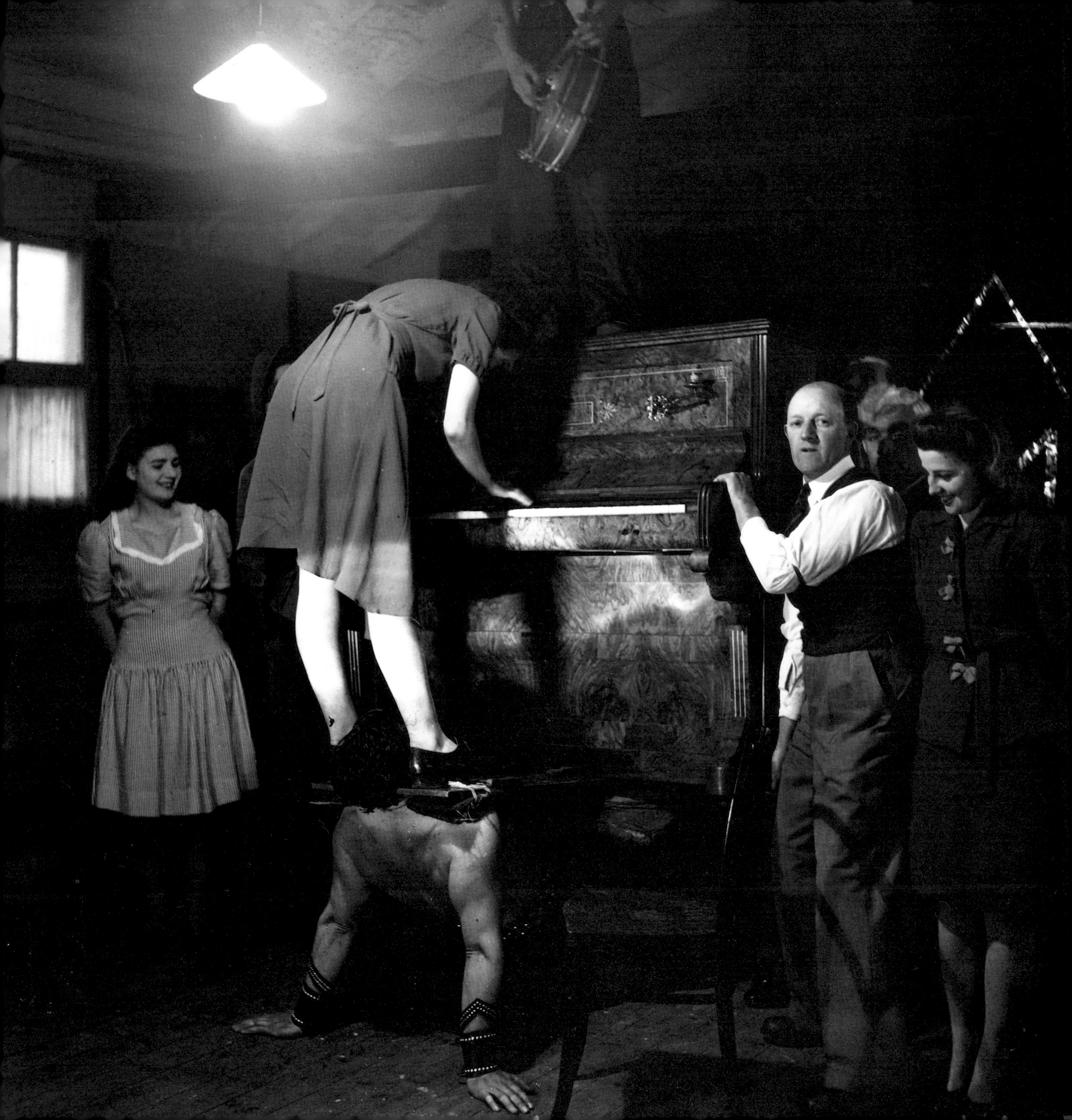

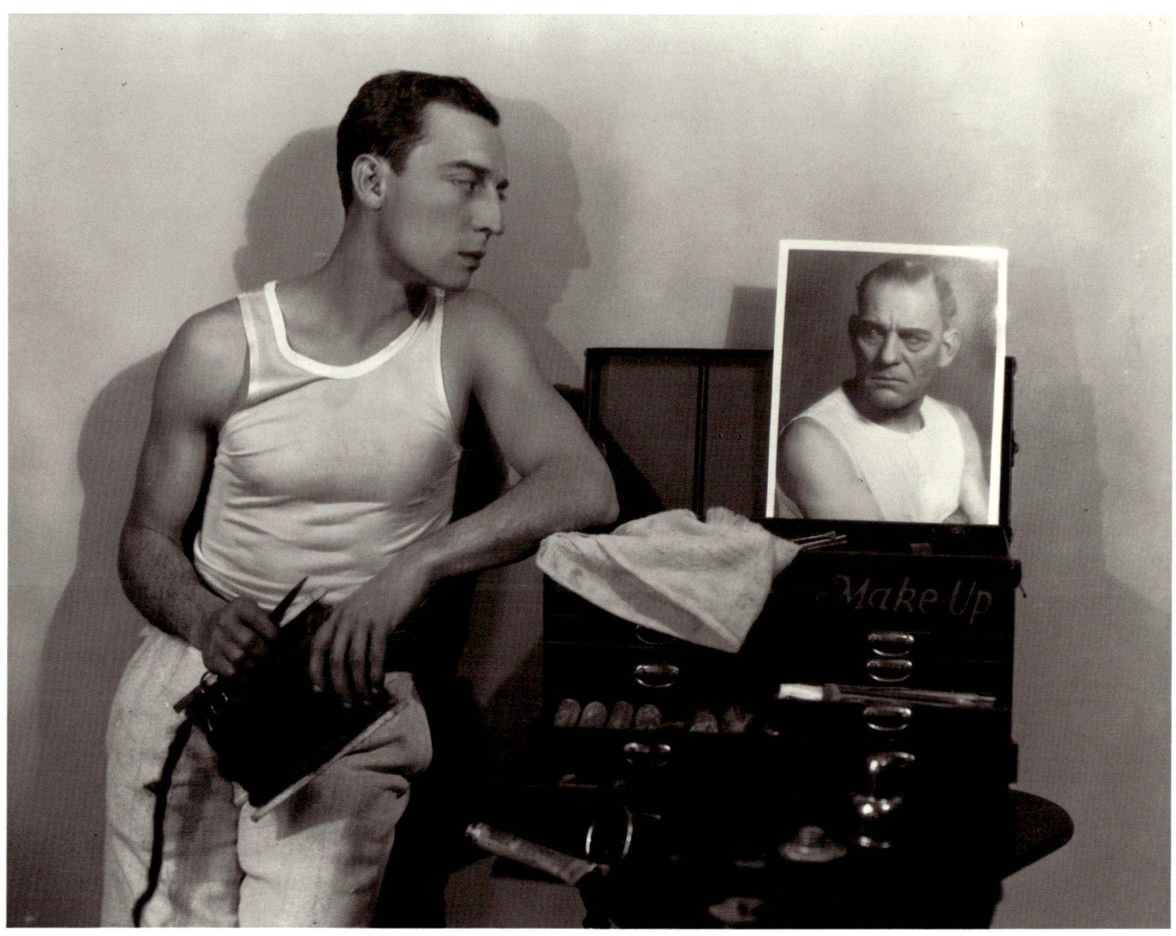

Ruth Harriet Louise, Metro Goldwyn Mayer
Buster Keaton, *undated*
'You see' said Buster, 'I'm just starting to work over here at
MGM and I've been sort of wondering if a new characterisation
wouldn't improve this dead pan of mine . . . perhaps something
after Lon Chaney's stuff.'

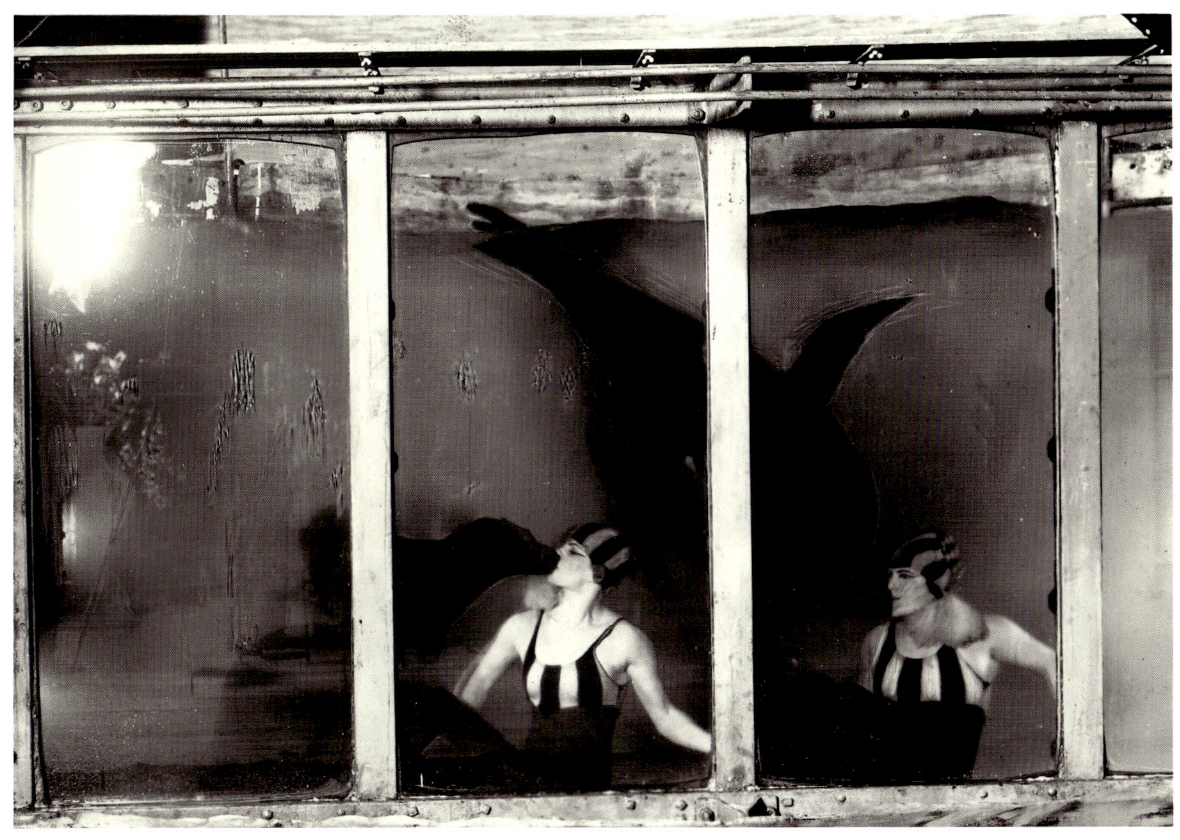

A. Gross, Berlin
Untitled, *1920s*

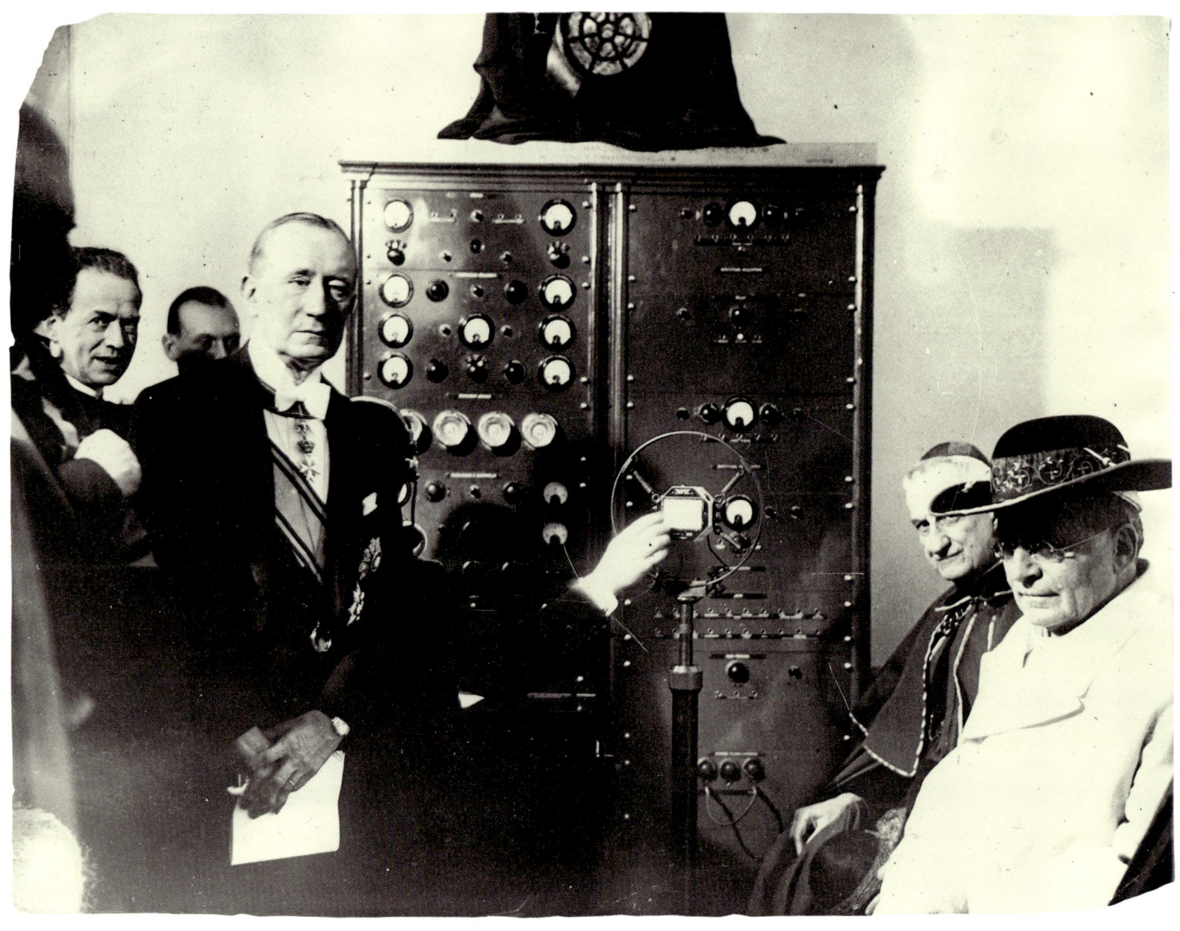

Photographer unknown, Planet News
The Vatican Radio Station, *1909*
Pope Pius XI listening to a speech of Marconi, who is standing in
front of a transmitting set.

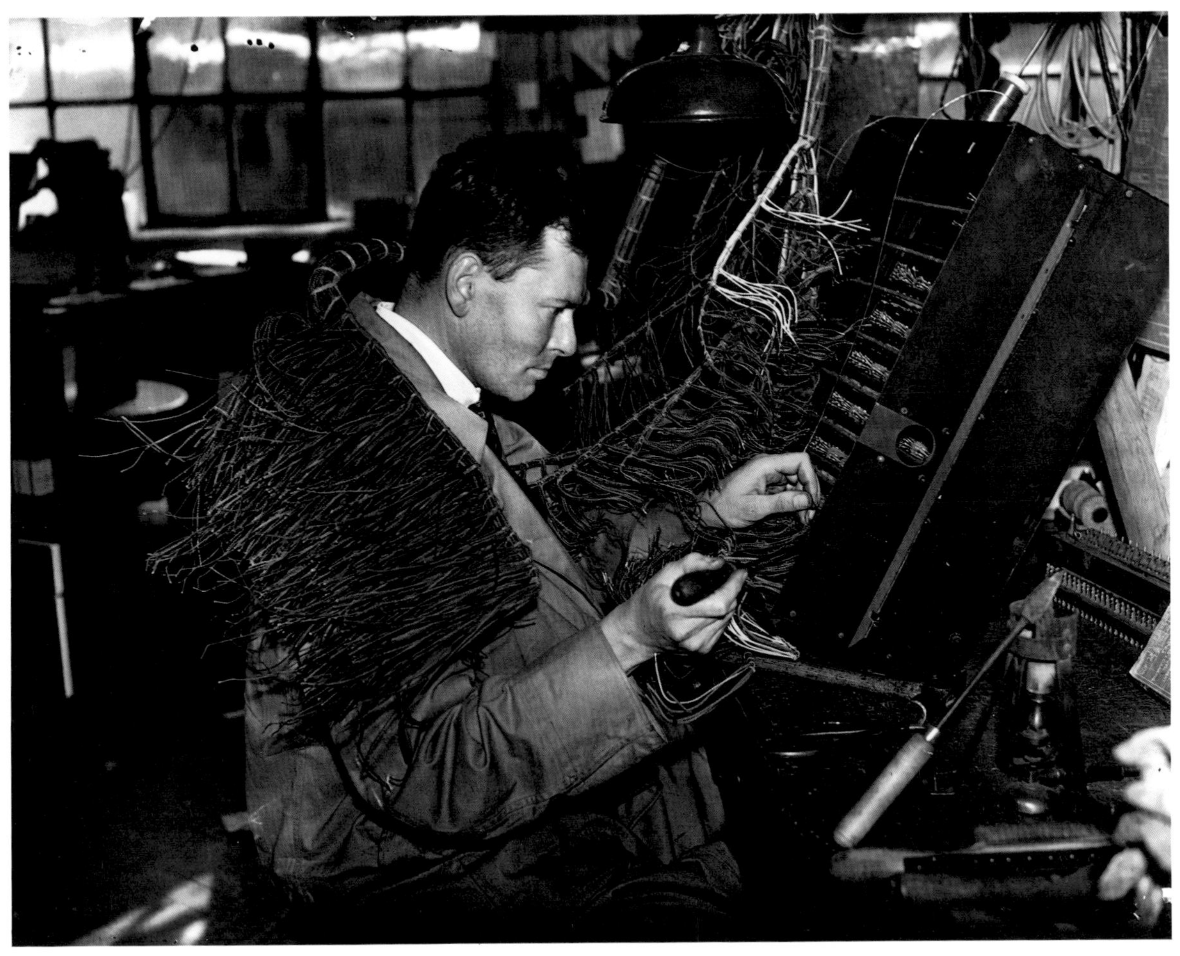

Photographer unknown, Fox Photos
GPO clock and telephone workshop at Holloway, *October 1937*

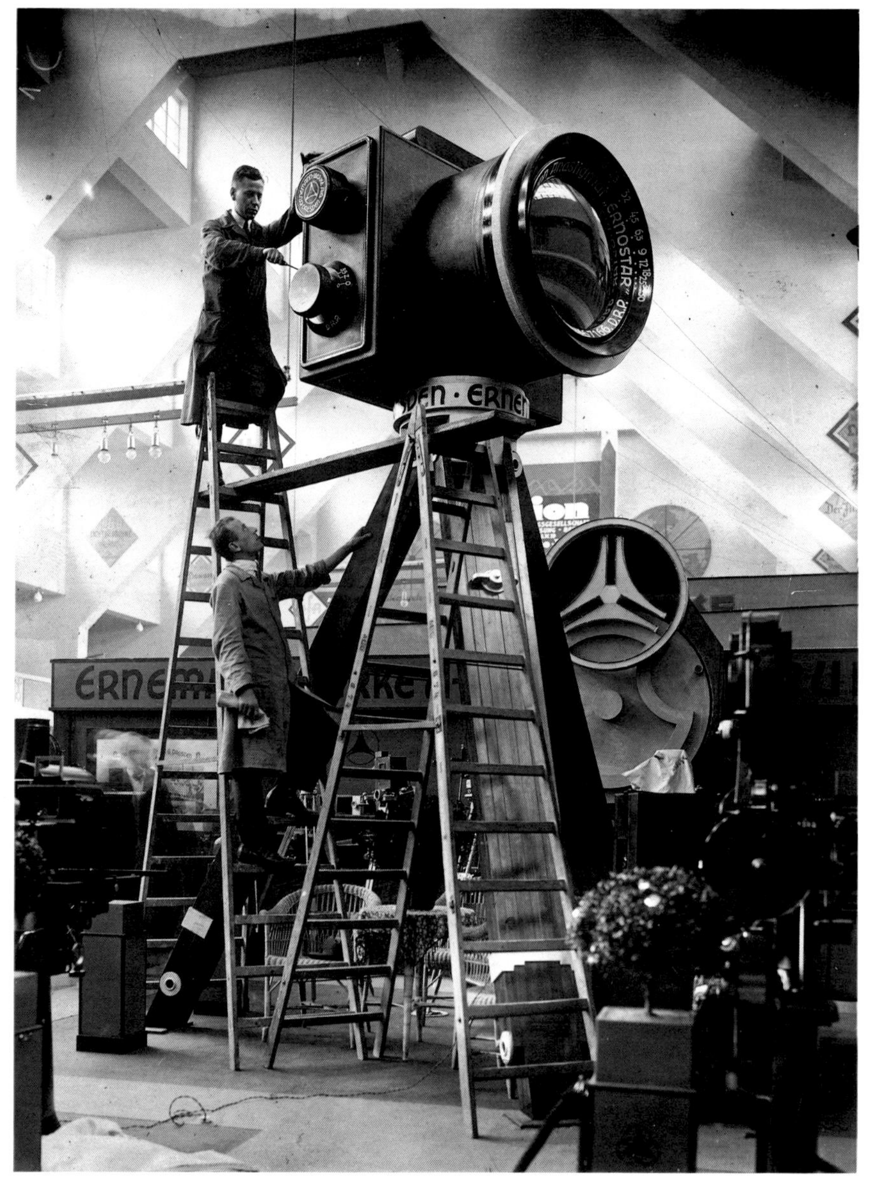

Photographer unknown
Opening of the 'Kipho cinema and photo-errection' Berlin, *1930s*

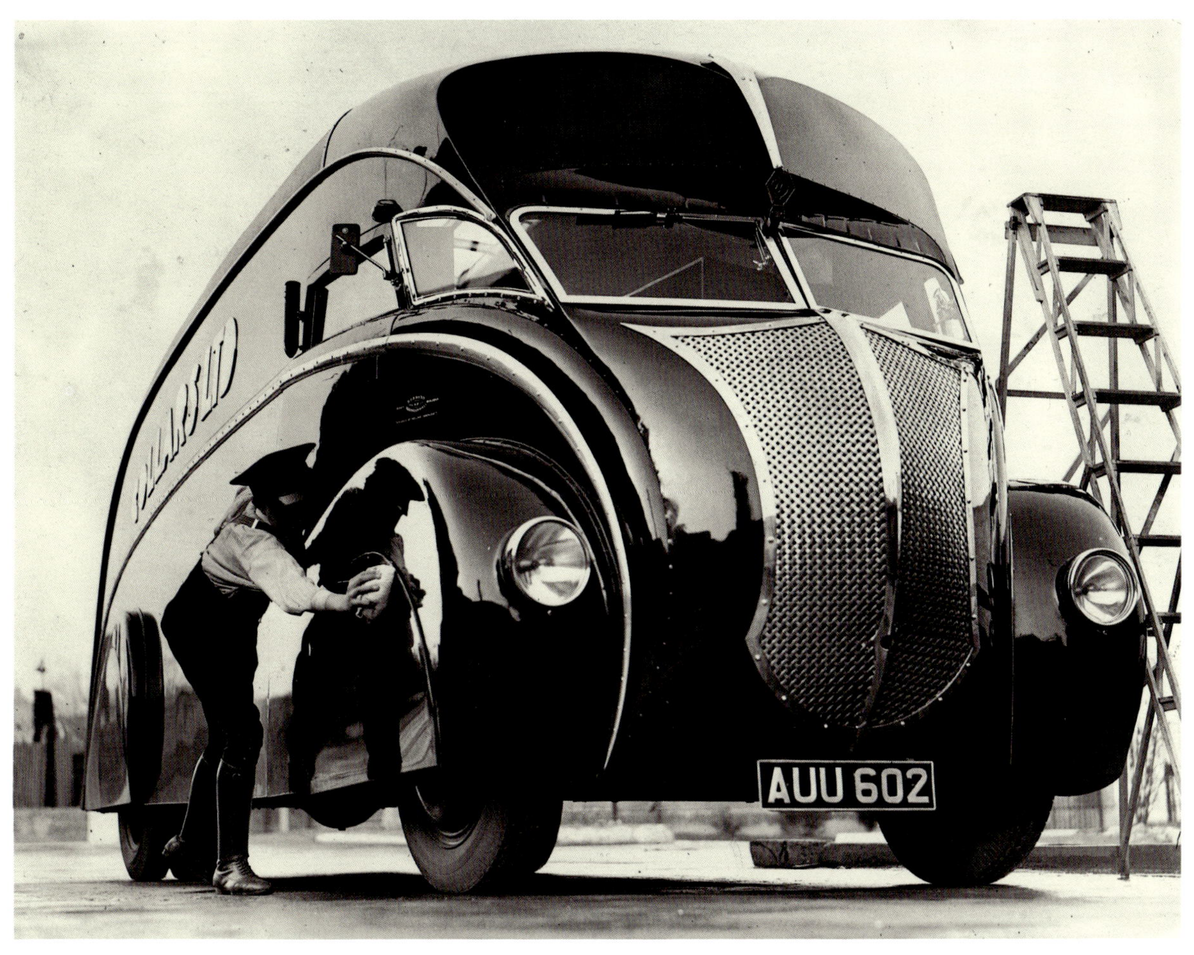

Photographer unknown, Fox Photos
Streamlined Van, Wembley, *1930s*

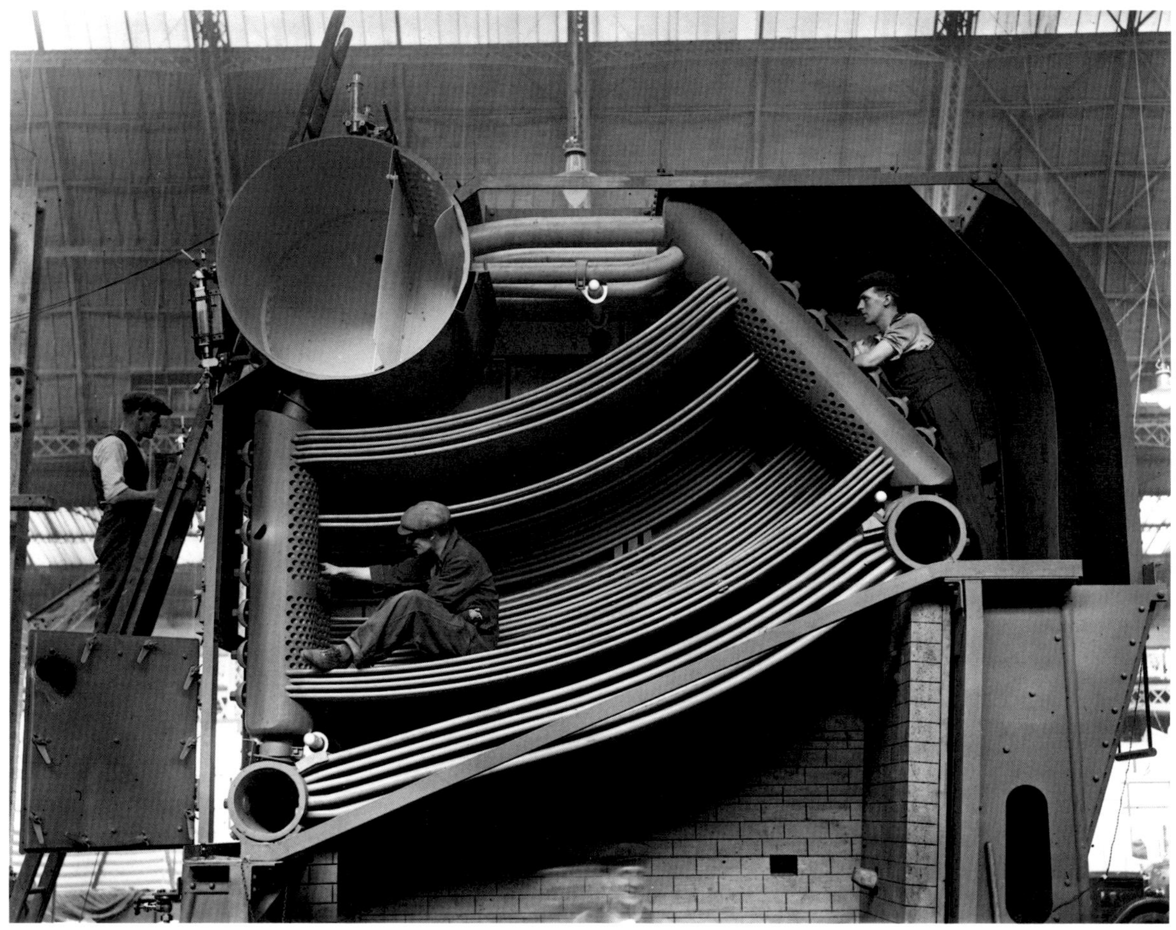

Photographer unknown, Topical Press
**Workmen completing a section of a high pressure steam boiler for a
shipping, engineering and machinery exhibition, Olympia, London,**
6 September 1933

Photographer unknown, Keystone
Teaching the Sudanese how to run their own railways, *1952*

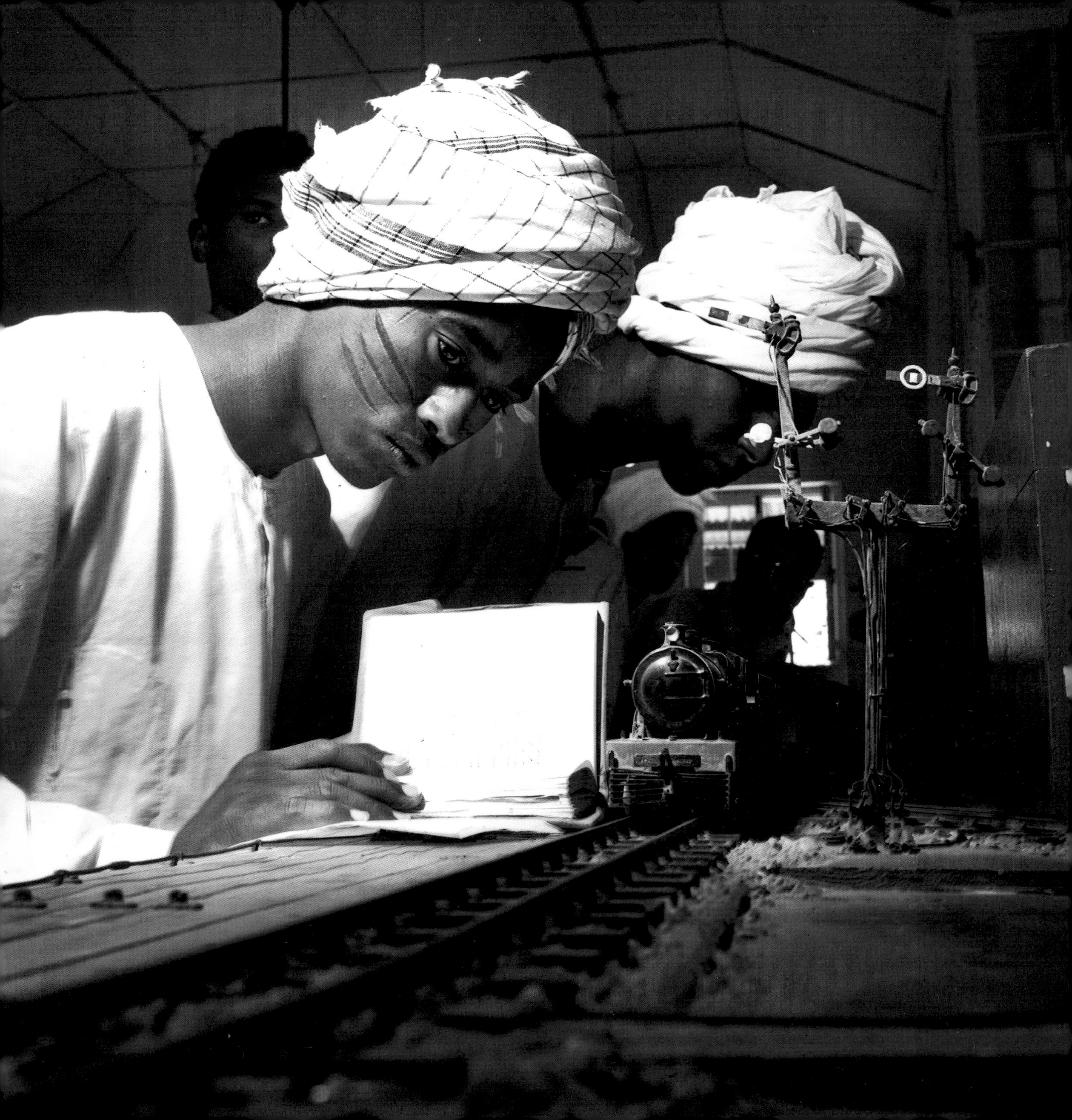

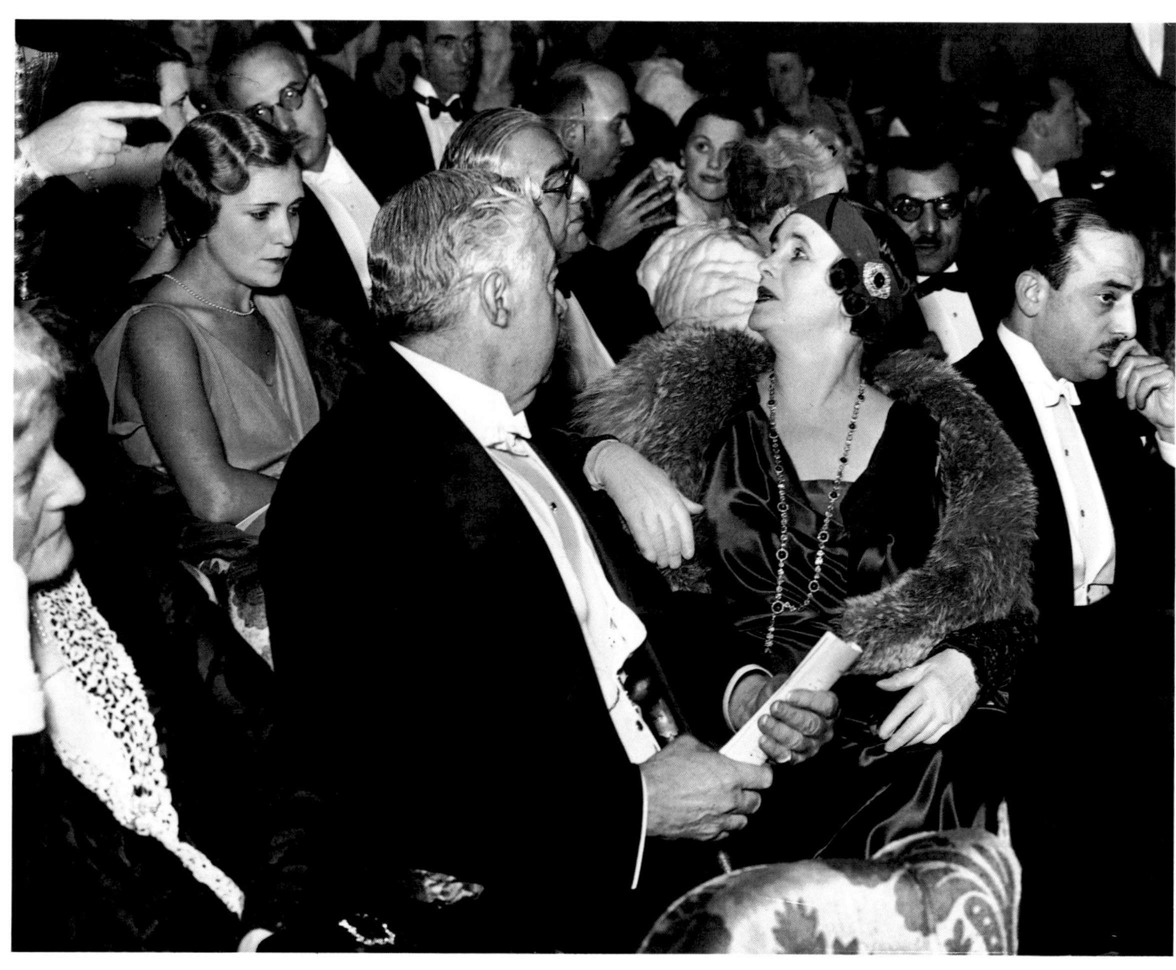

Photographer unknown, Topical Press
Little Catherine – First Night, Phoenix Theatre, *1931*

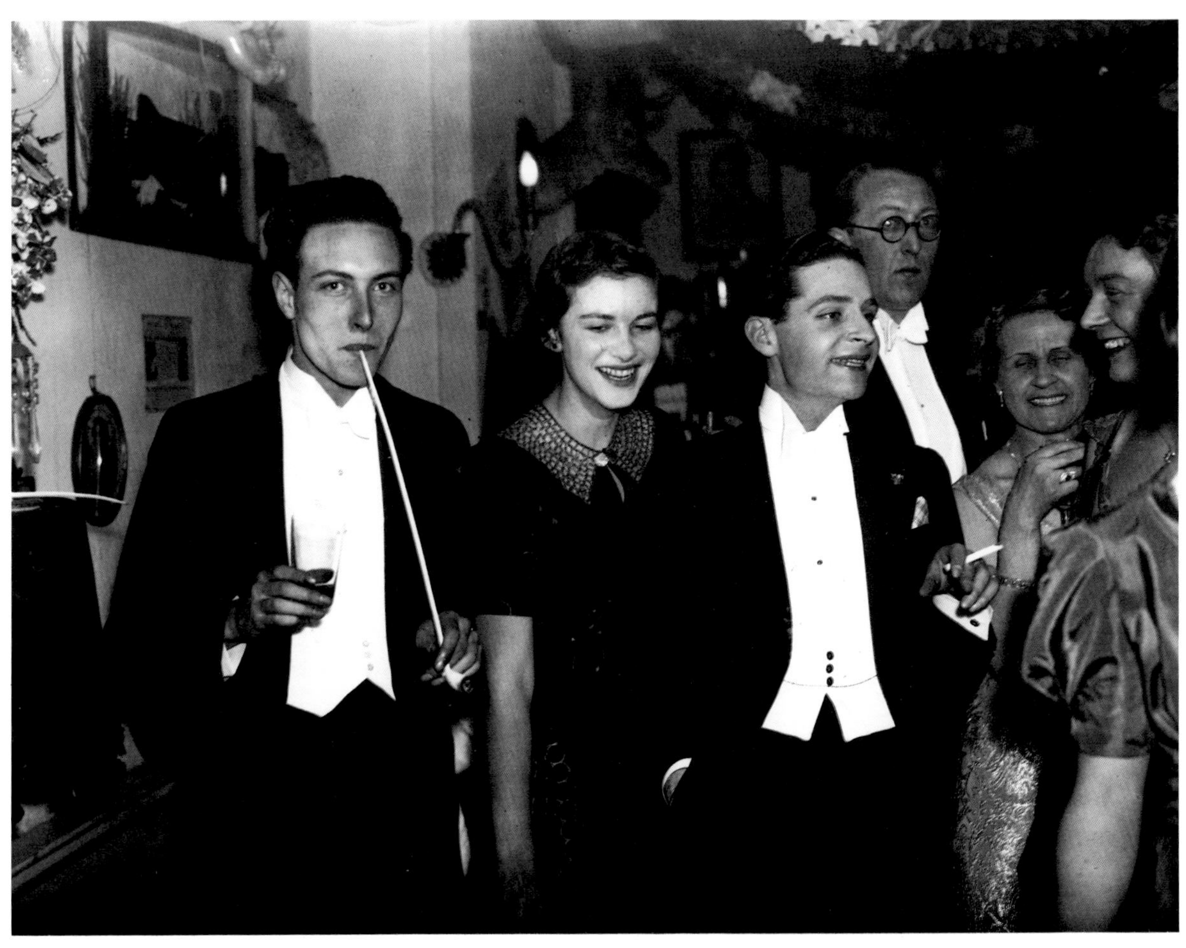

Photographer unknown, Topical Press
Ball at Lullingstone Castle, Kent, *19 February 1938*

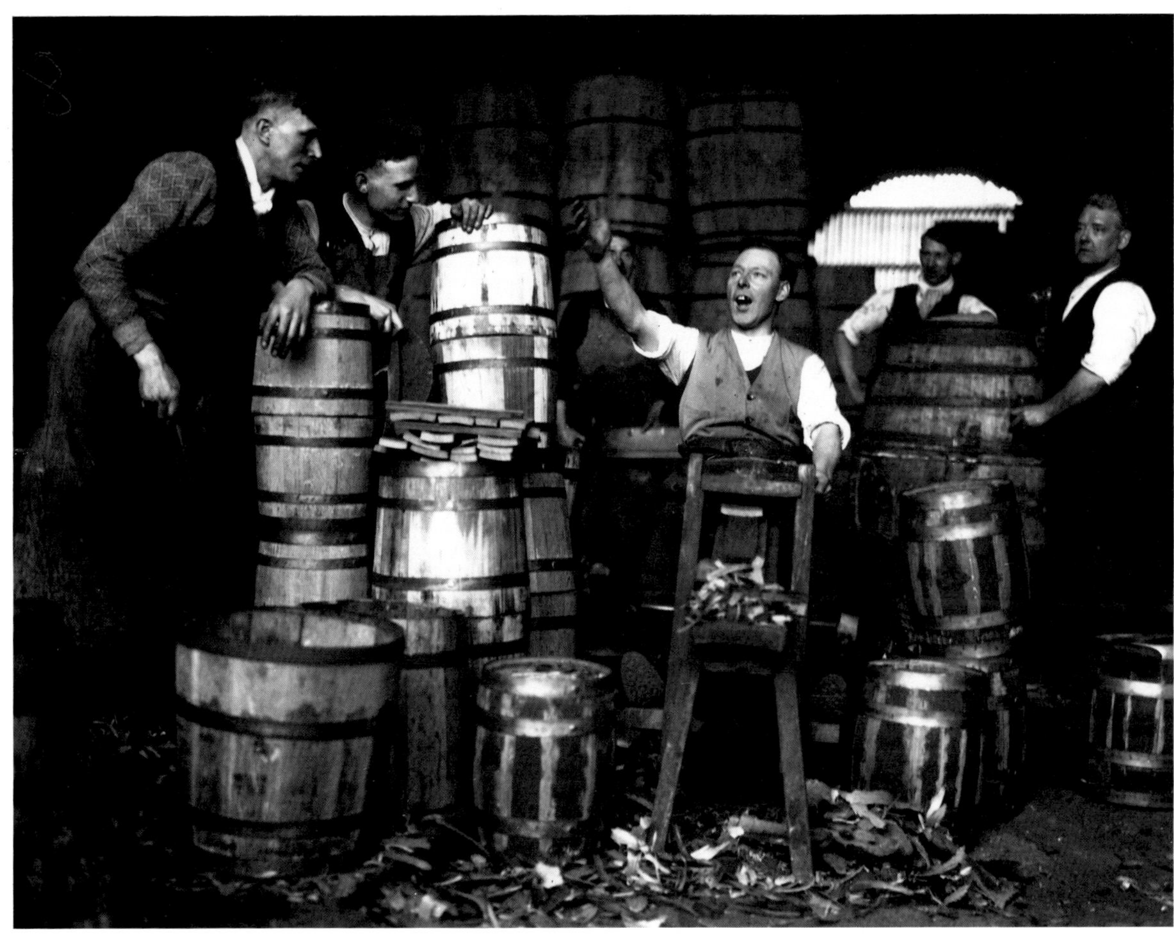

Photographer unknown, Topical Press
The Singing Cooper – he sings as he makes his barrels, *March 1935*

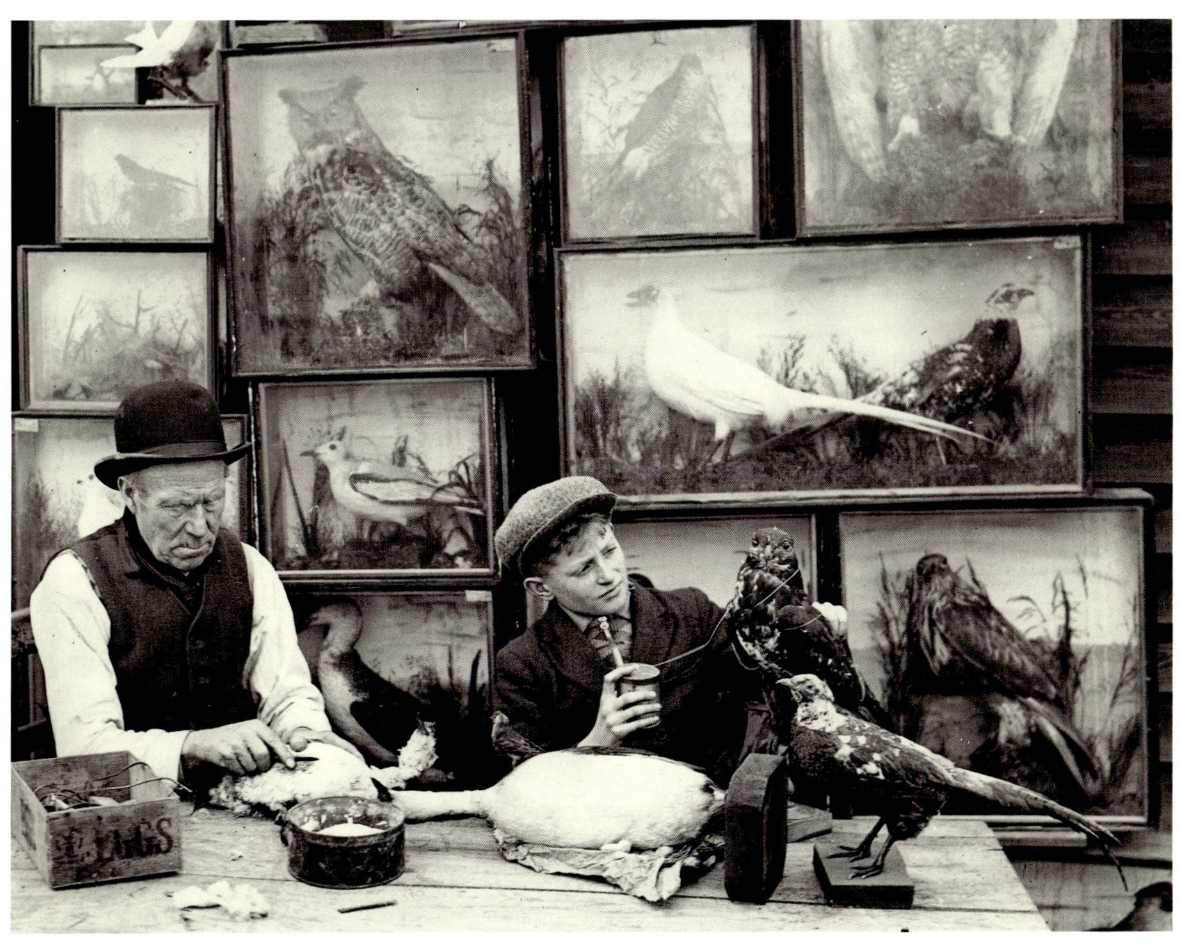

Photographer unknown, Fox Photos
Old Man's Hobby in Broken Down Shed, *8 February 1933*
Mr. Thomas Sparrow, a 72 year old bird collector and his grandson at work.

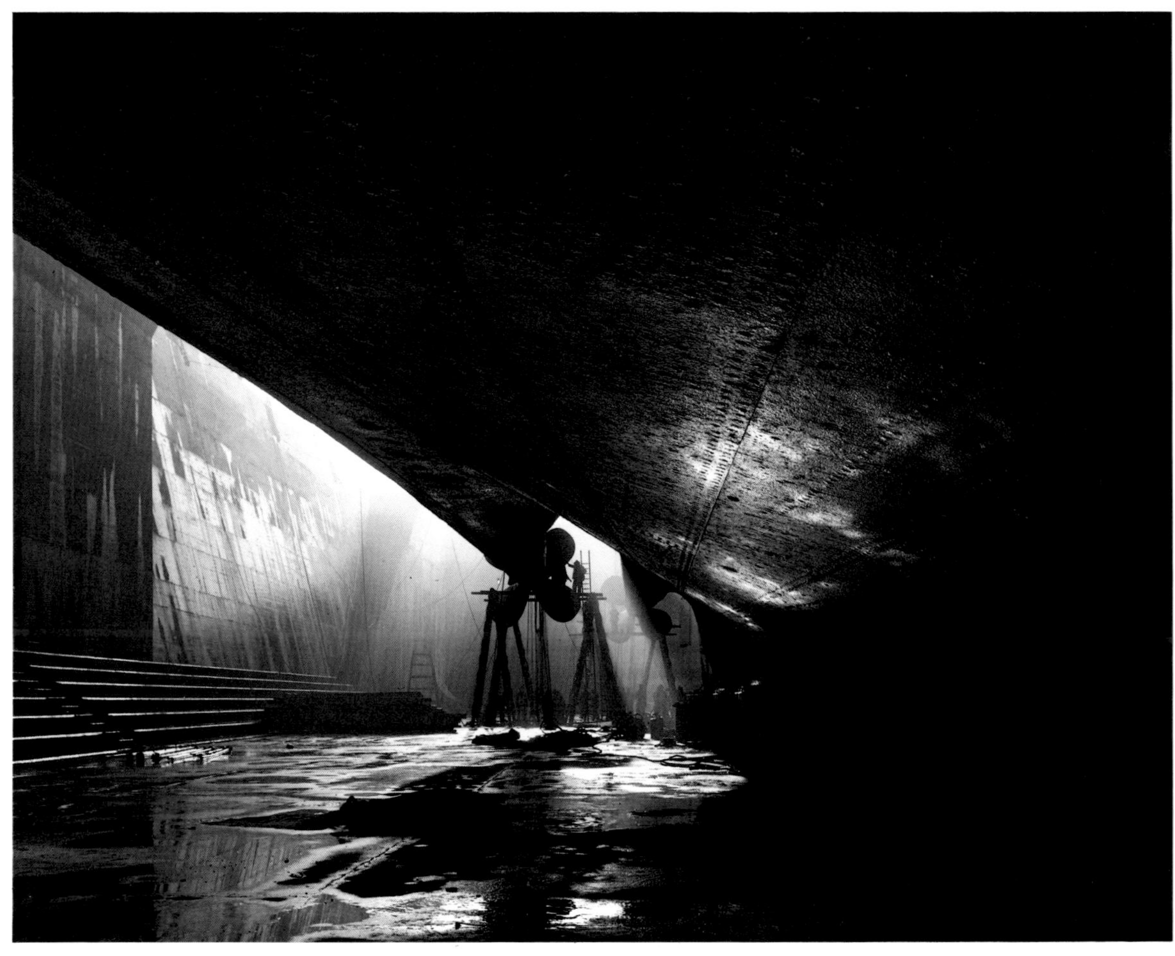

Photographer unknown, Topical Press
Underneath Britain's Largest Liner, *22 January 1934*
A view of the propellers of the 'Majestic', taken from the keel
blocks of the world's largest graving-dock at Southampton.

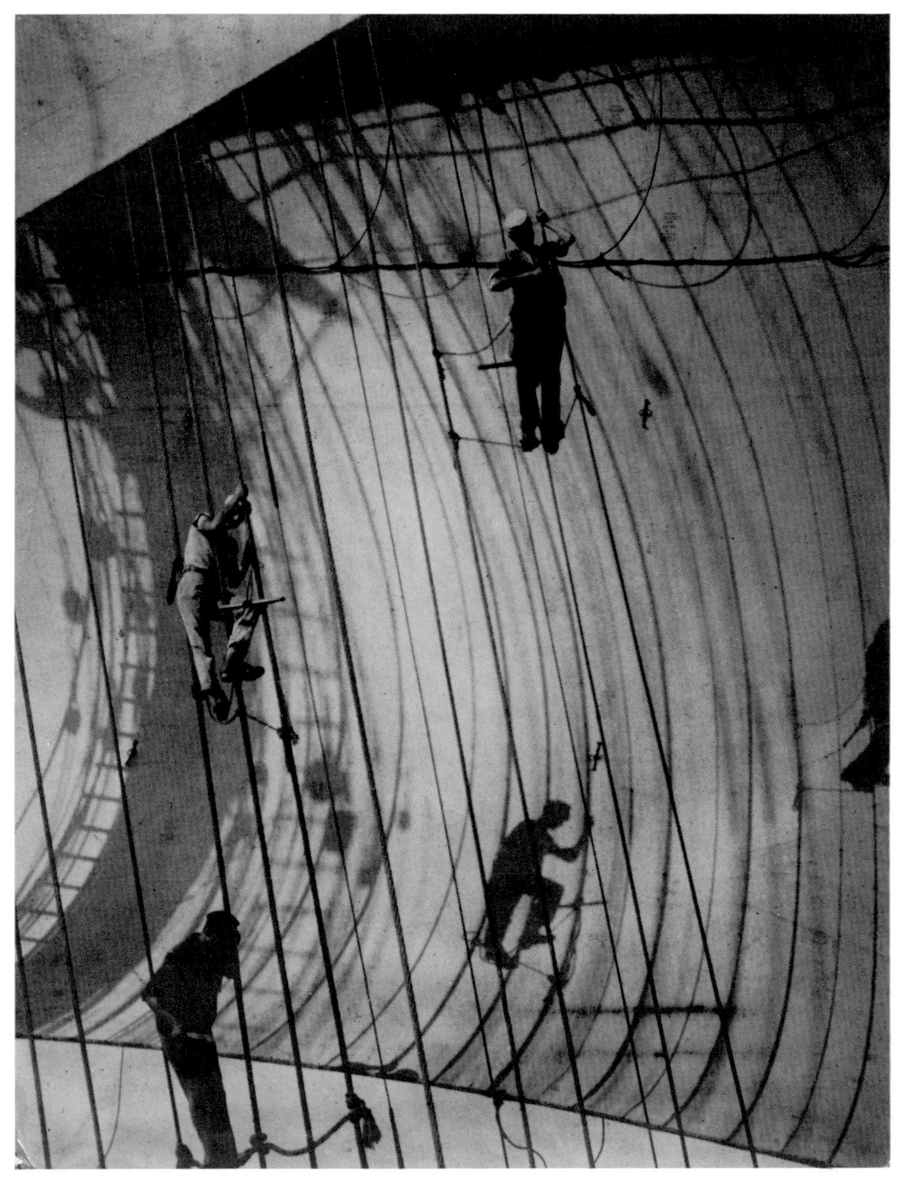

Photographer unknown
'On board a windjammer – The Parma', *c1930*

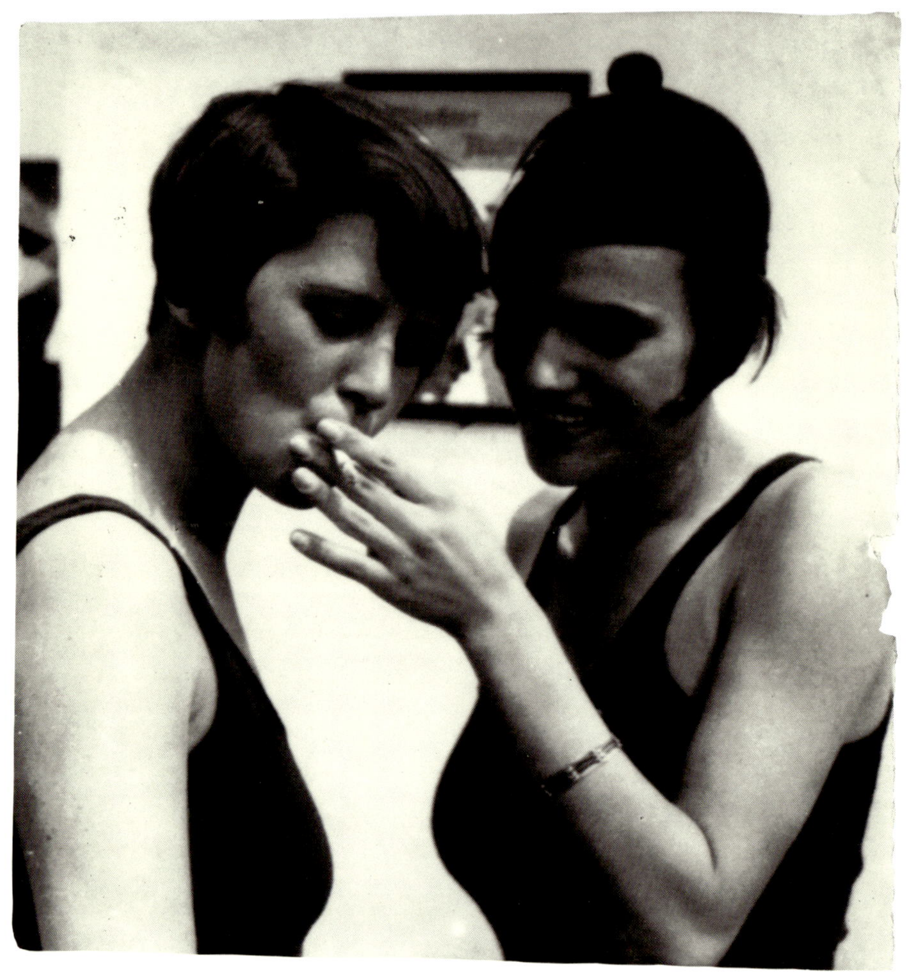

Photographer unknown, Guttmann Agency
Untitled, *c1930 (possibly Germany)*

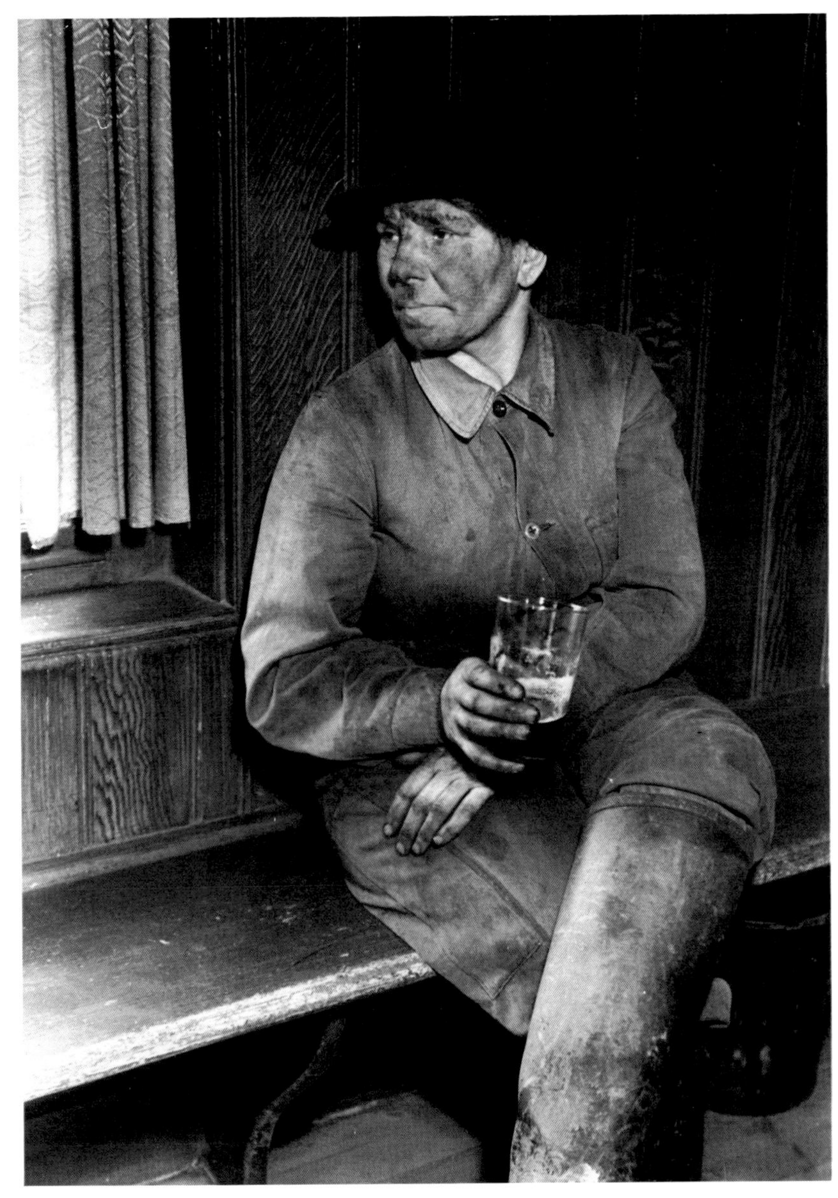

George Douglas,
Olive Walker, Lady Sweep, *Picture Post, 21 April 1951*

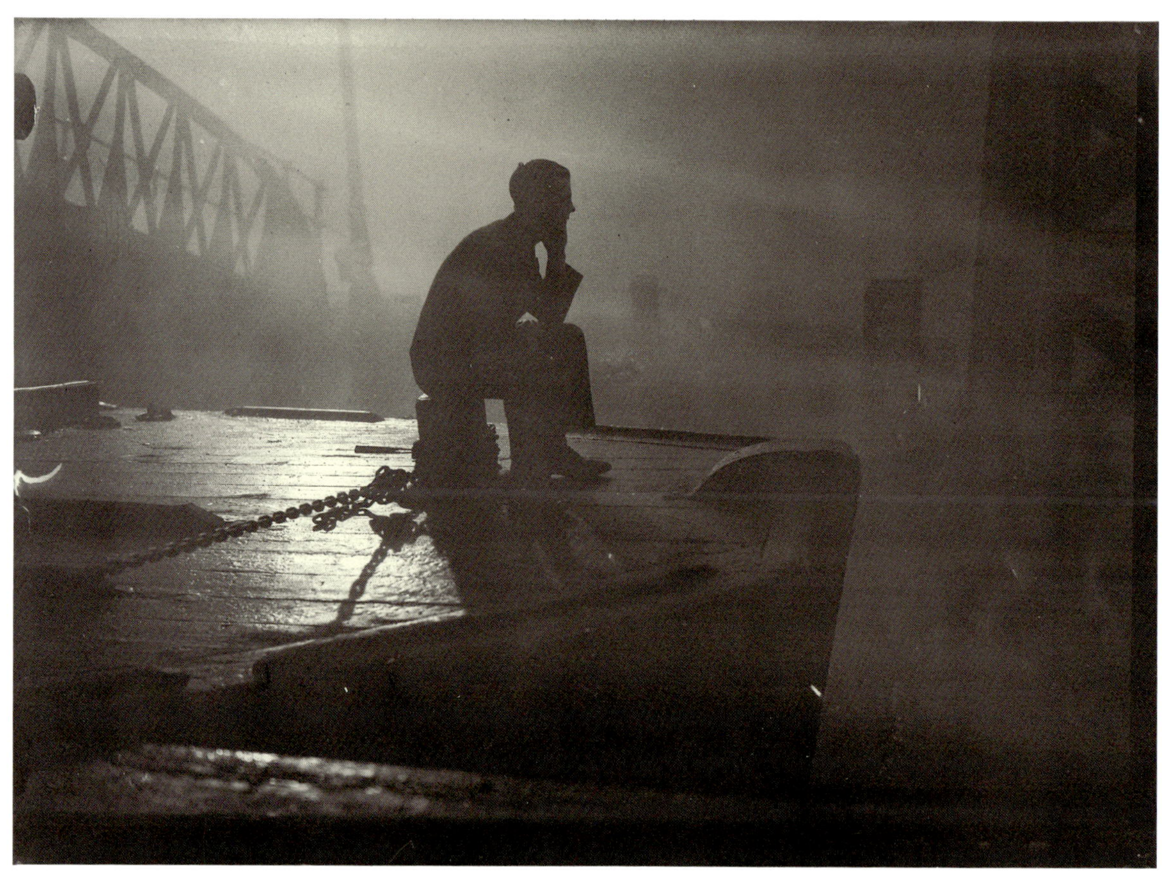

Photographer unknown, Topical Press
London Fogbound, *30 November 1931*
'A London bargee on the Thames patiently waiting on the stern
of his barge for the fog to lift.'

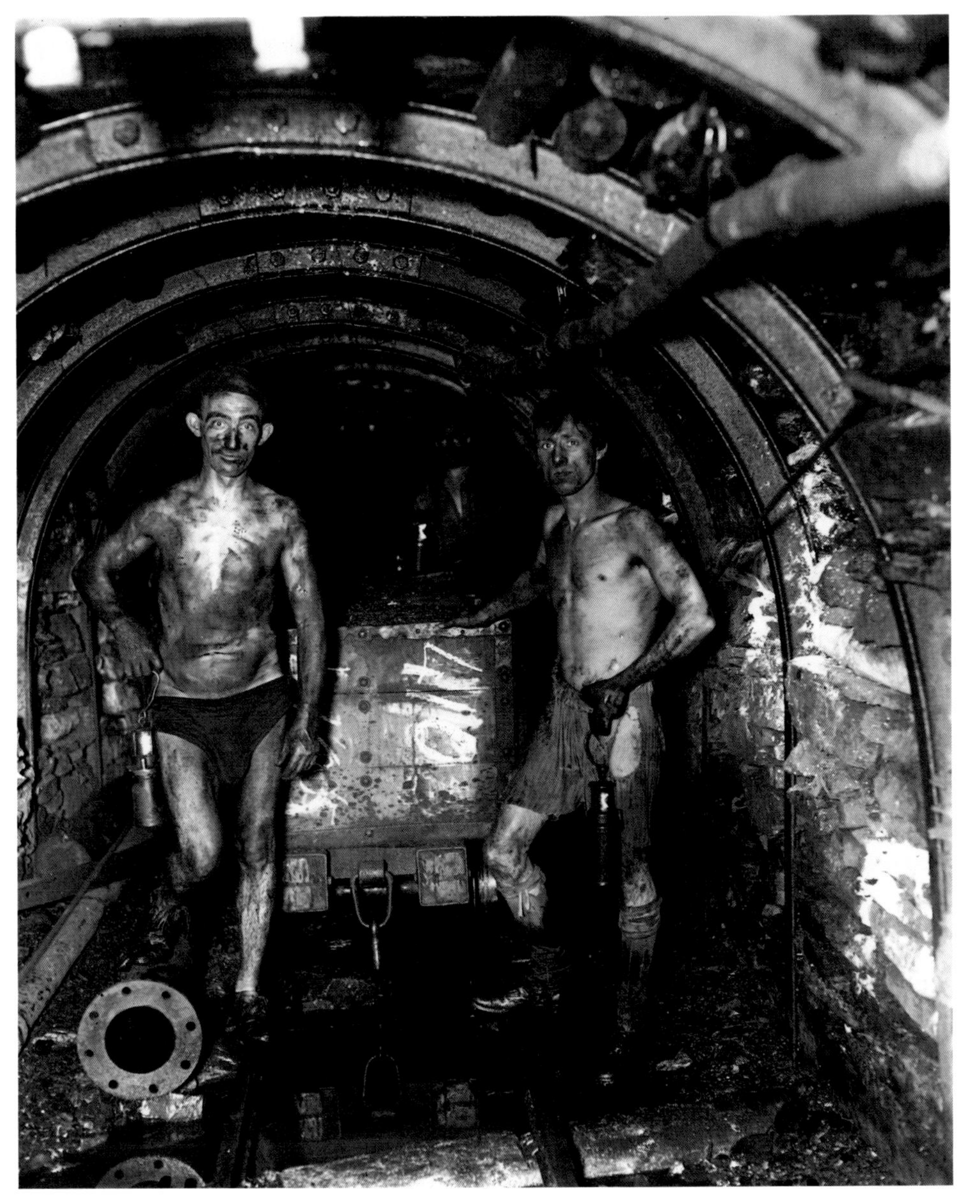

Sasha
Tilmanstone Colliery, Kent, *June 1930*

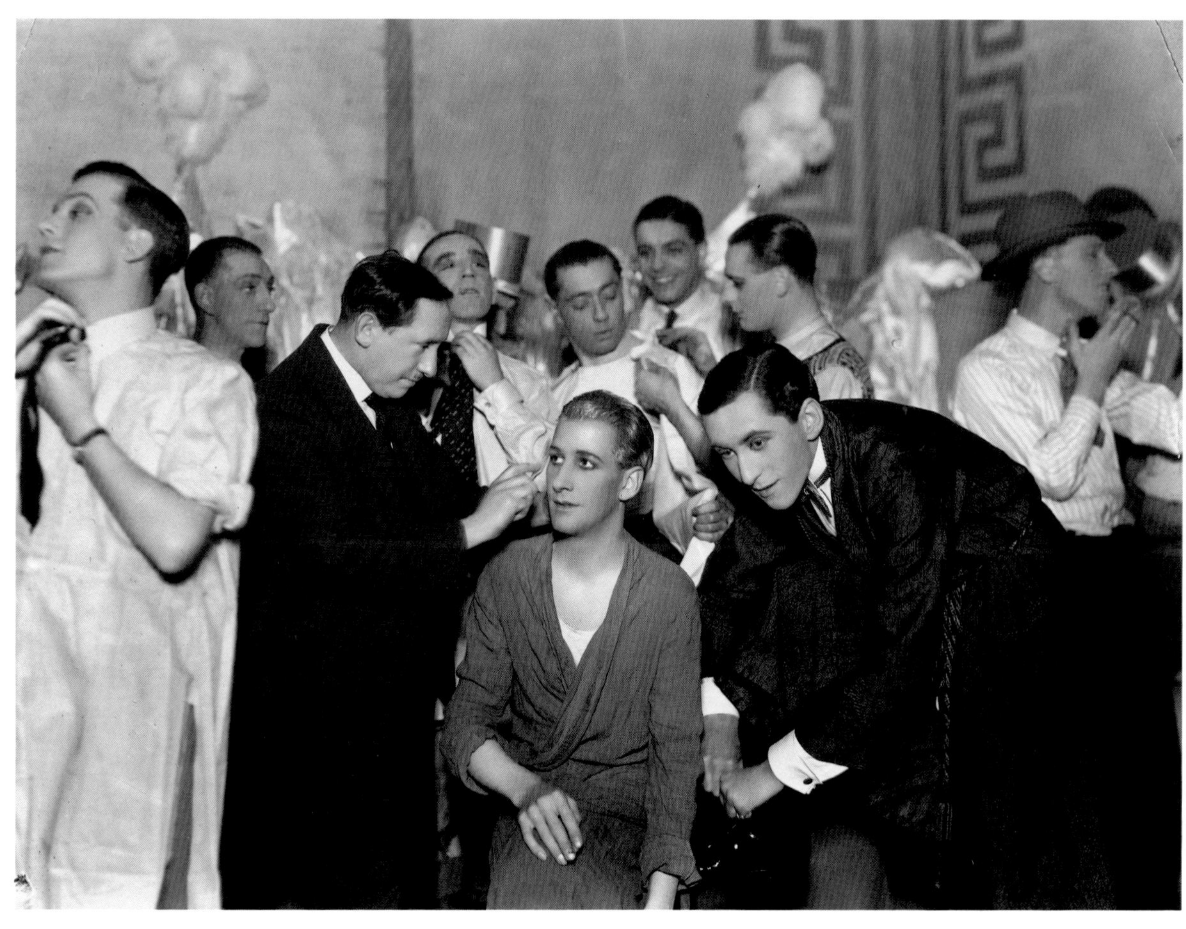

Sasha
Chorus boys being made up for the production of 'Evergreen' at the Adelphi Theatre, *1930*

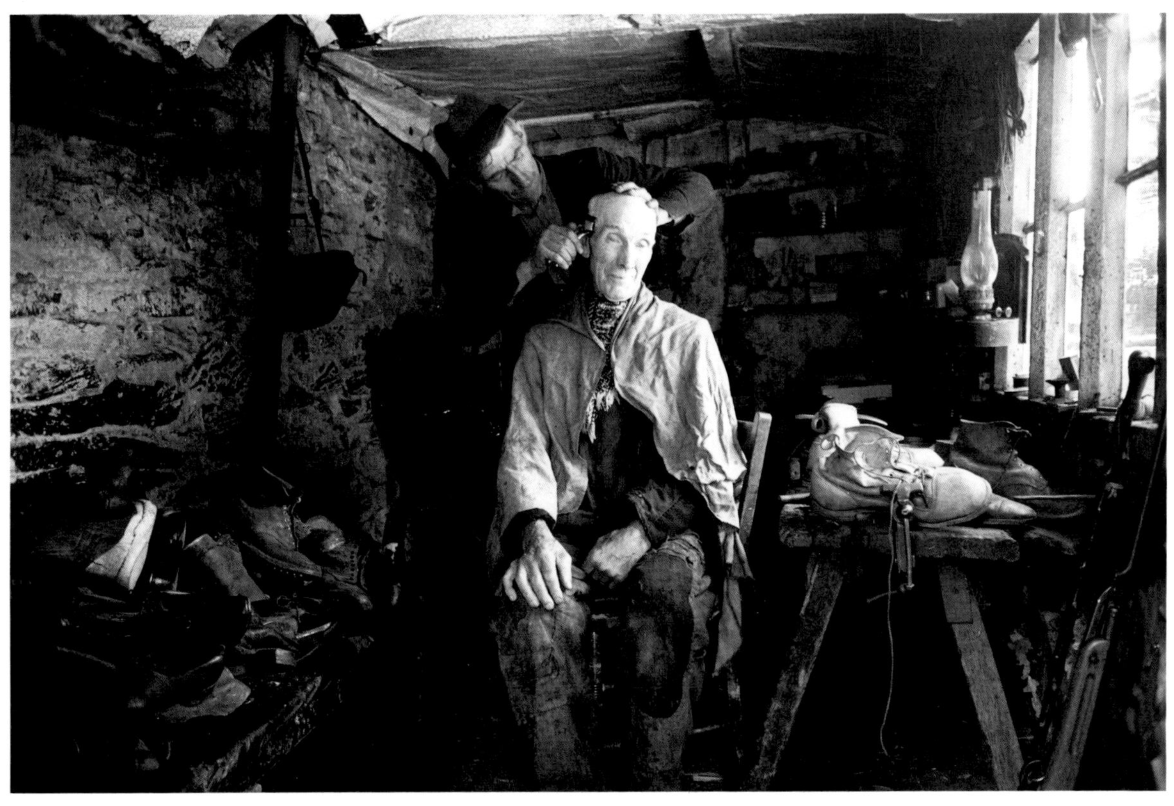

Kurt Hutton
A Man of Hills and Rivers – the story of the countryside of Robert Gibbings author and artist, *14 October 1944*
'It's Handel Lewis again, cutting the hair of ''Old Tom'' Owen, the hedge-laying specialist. Handel's other jobs are farmer's help, chimney sweep, special constable, electric lighting engineer, and mender of the village shoes.'

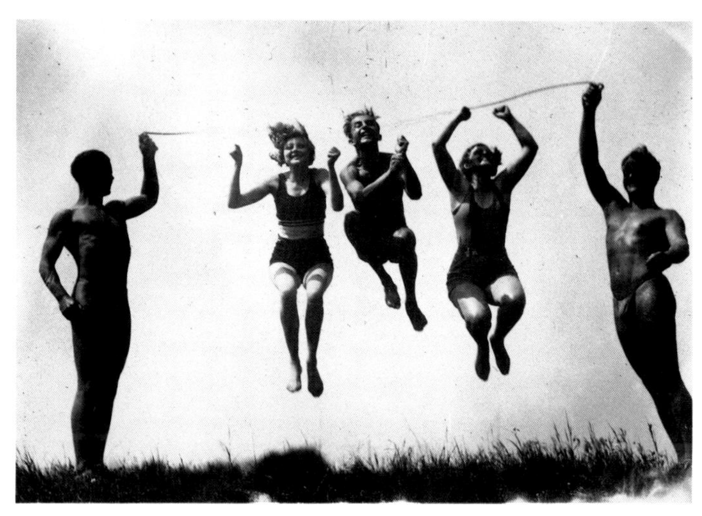

Photographer unknown, G.P.A.
Untitled, *c1925*

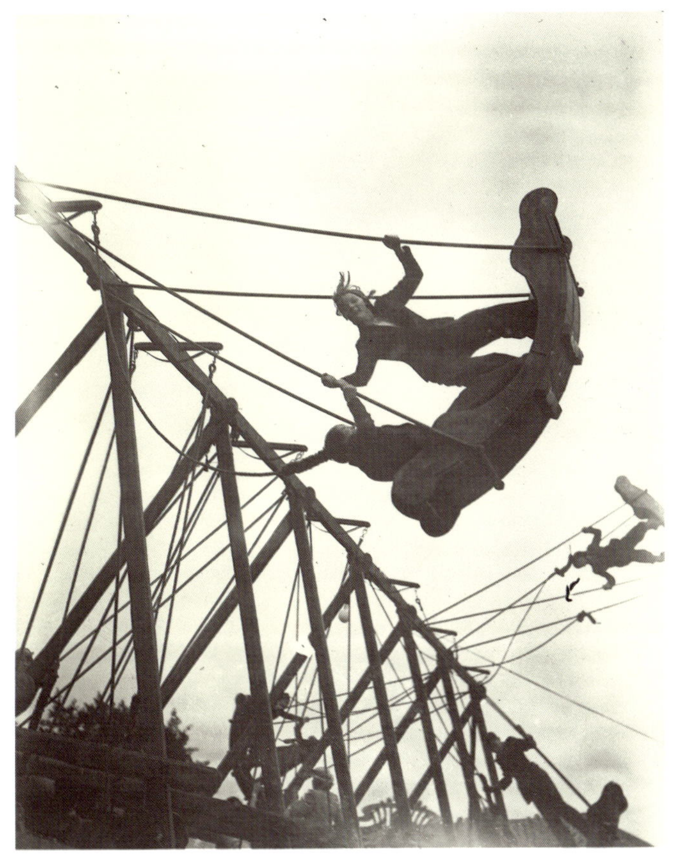

Photographer unknown, Topical Press
All the Fun O' the Fair, Hampstead Heath, *3 August 1936*

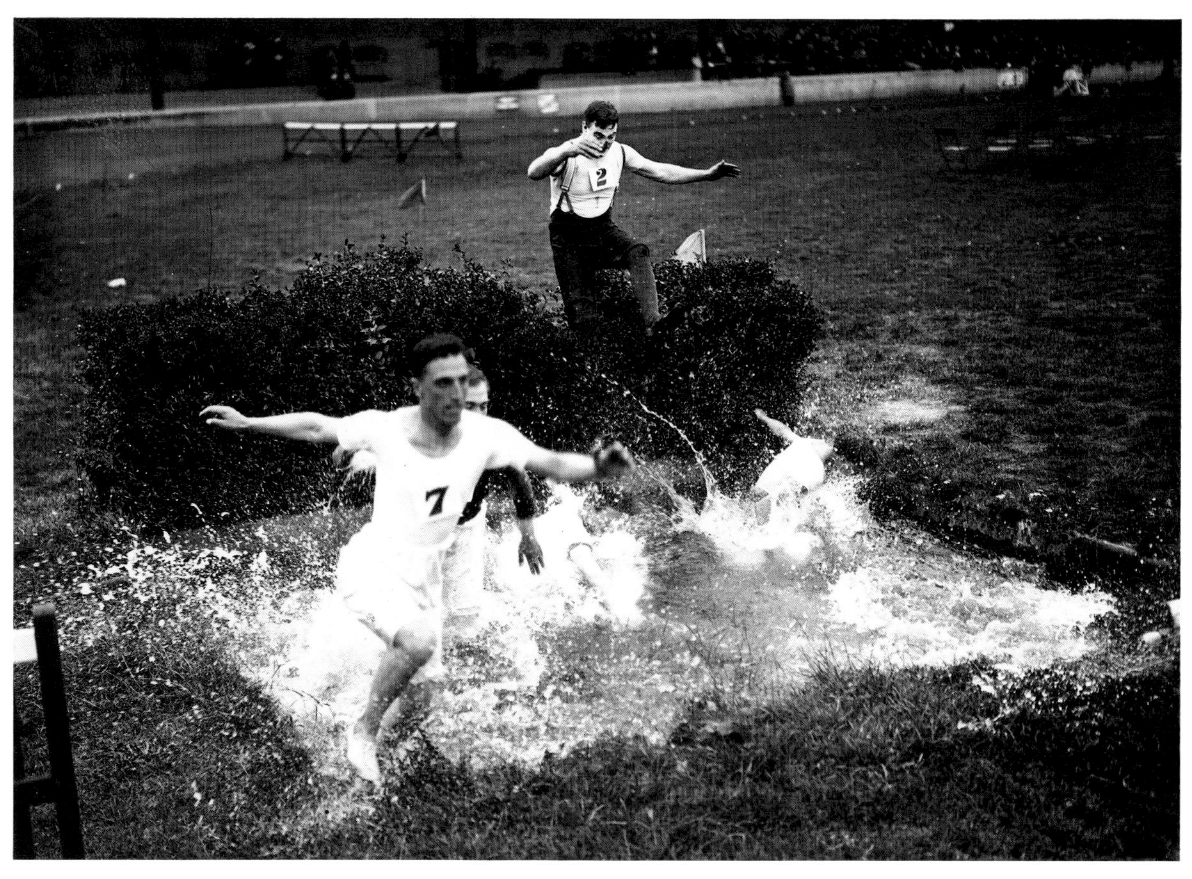

Photographer unknown
London Busmen's Sports at Stamford Bridge – Obstacle Race,
July 1920

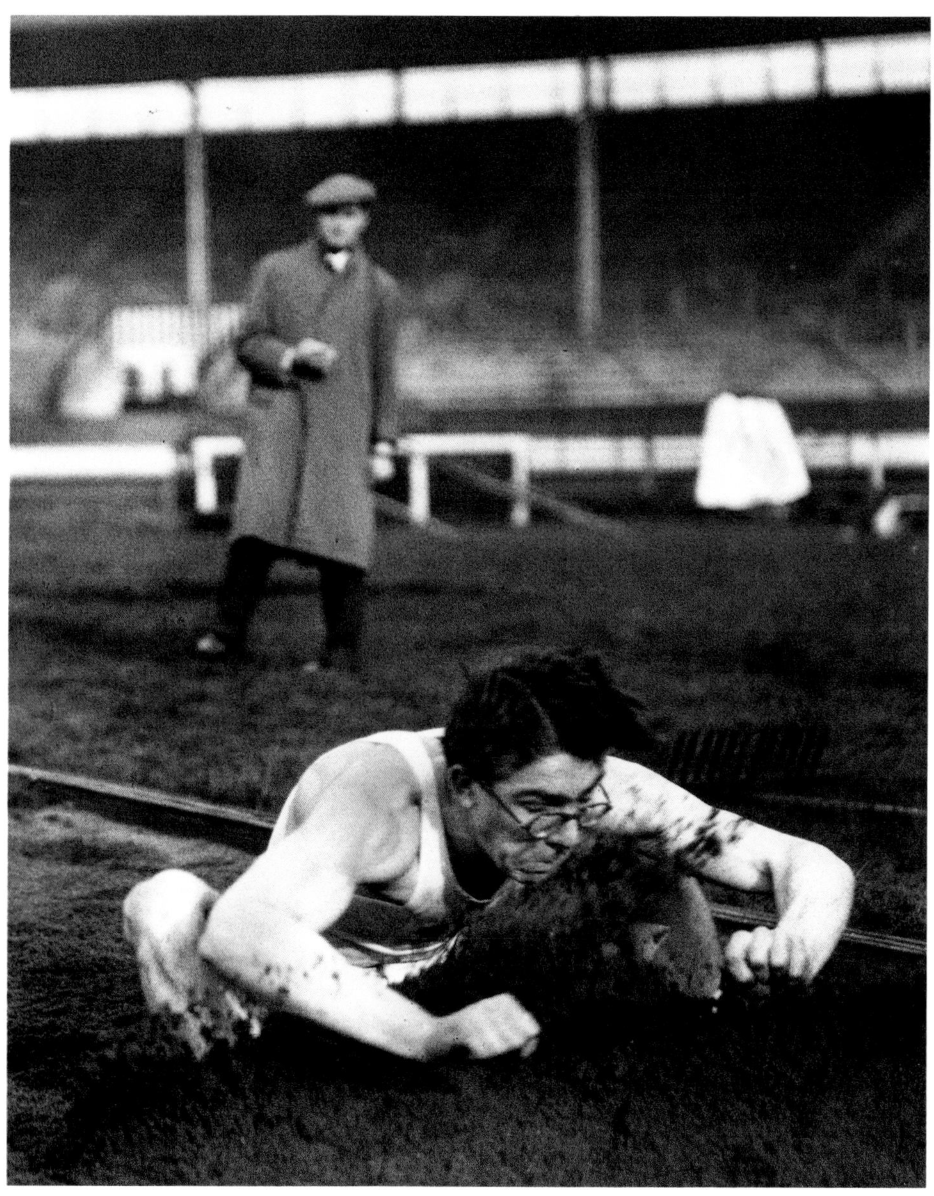

Photographer unknown, Topical Press
Varsity Athletes at the White City, *12 May 1937*

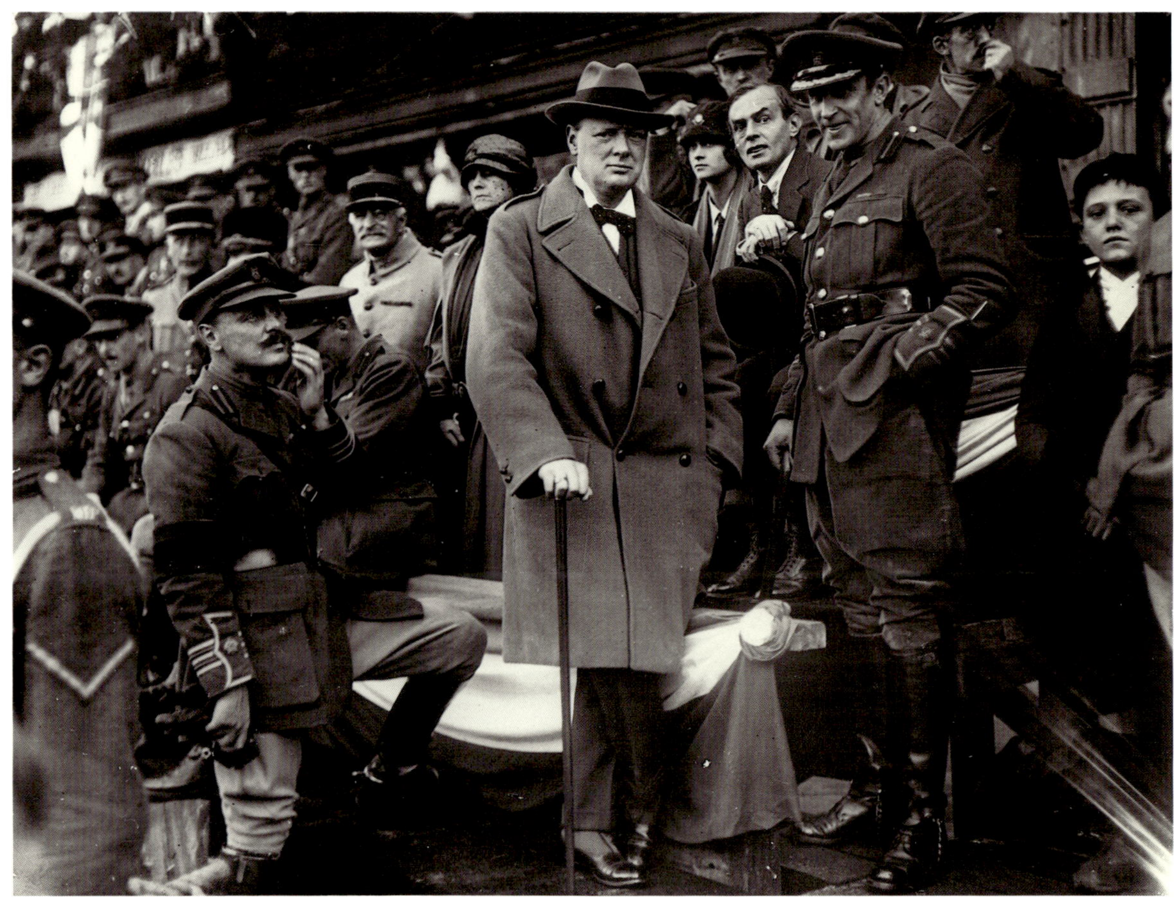

Photographer unknown

**The Secretary of State for War, Winston Churchill, on the Grand
Stand in the Grande Place at Lille watching the march past of the
47th Division**, *22 October 1918*

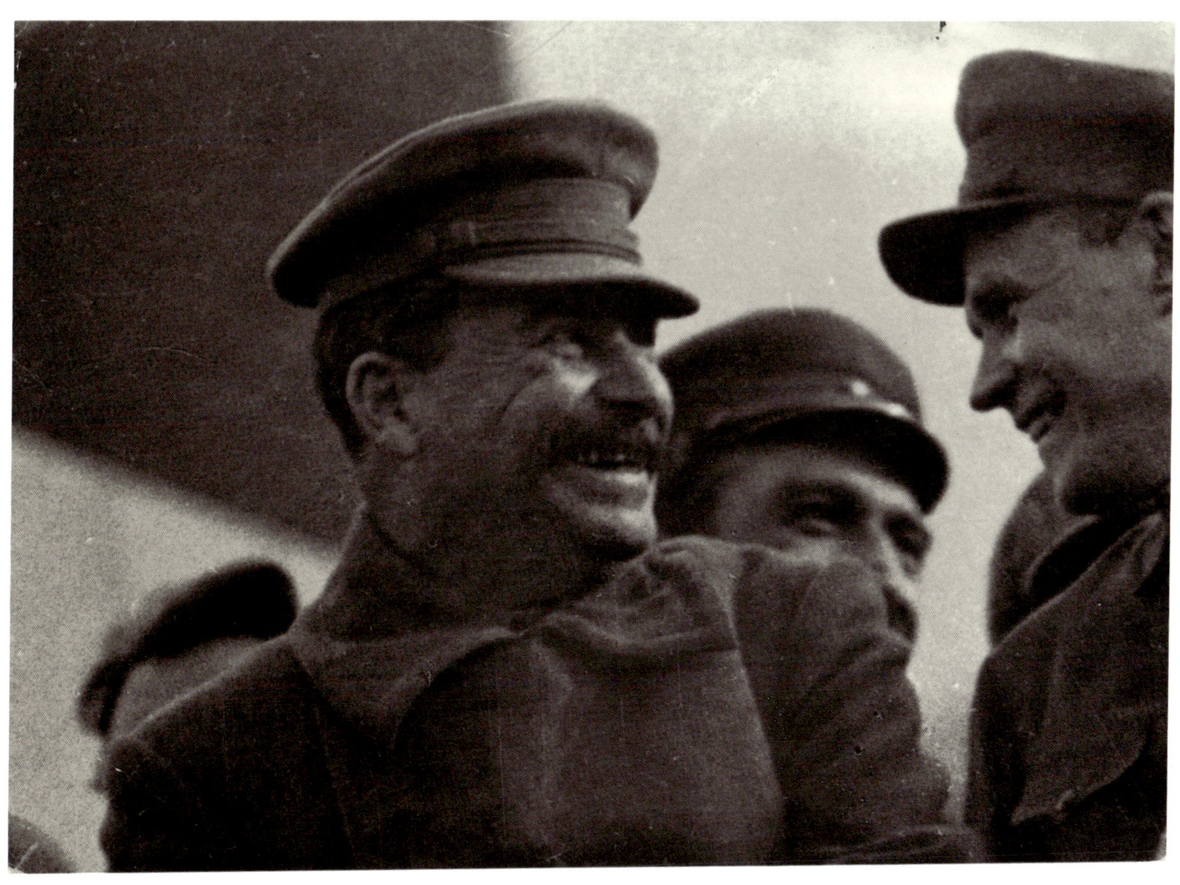

Photographer unknown, Planet News
Josef Stalin on the tribune during a parade of workers, *(undated)*

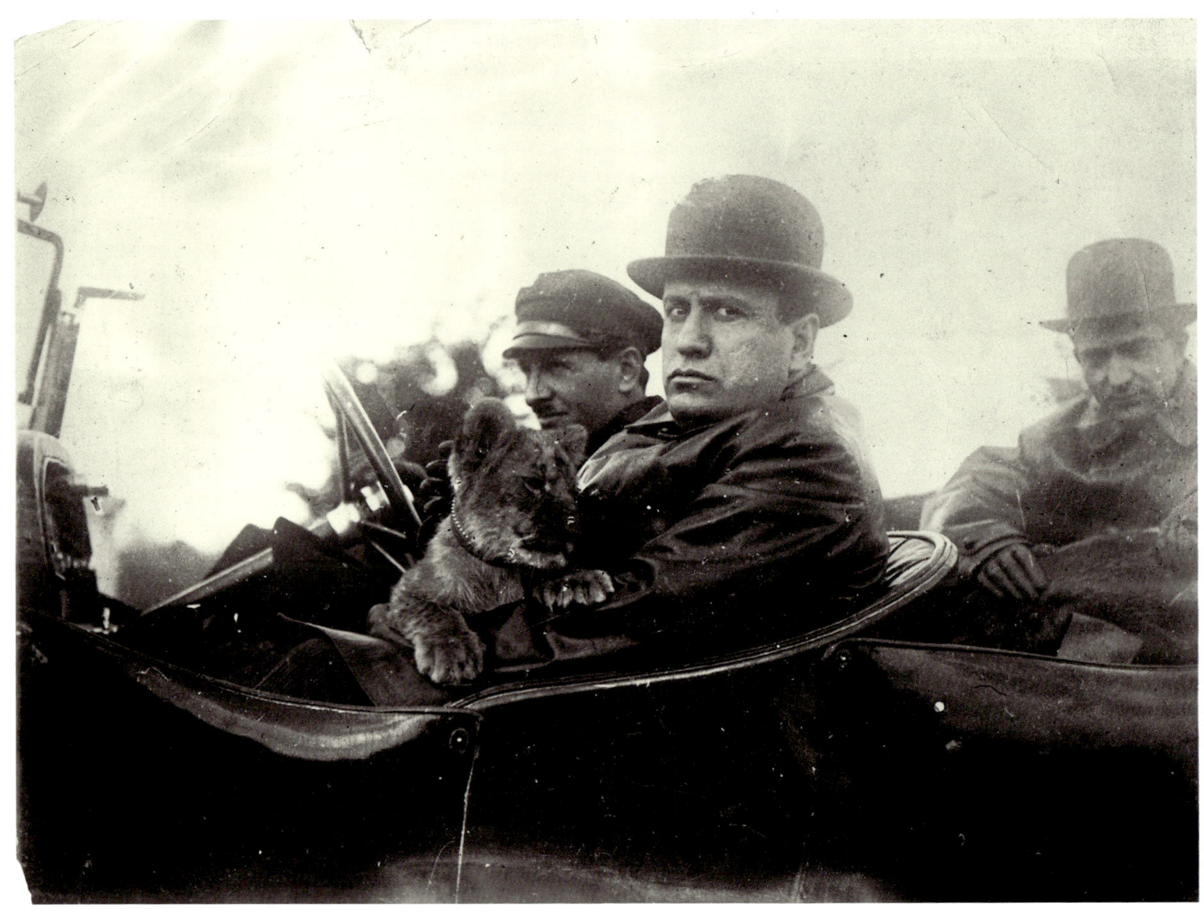

Photographer unknown, Keystone
**Premier Mussolini of Italy with his pet tiger cub,
a gift from Aldo Finci**, *c1925*

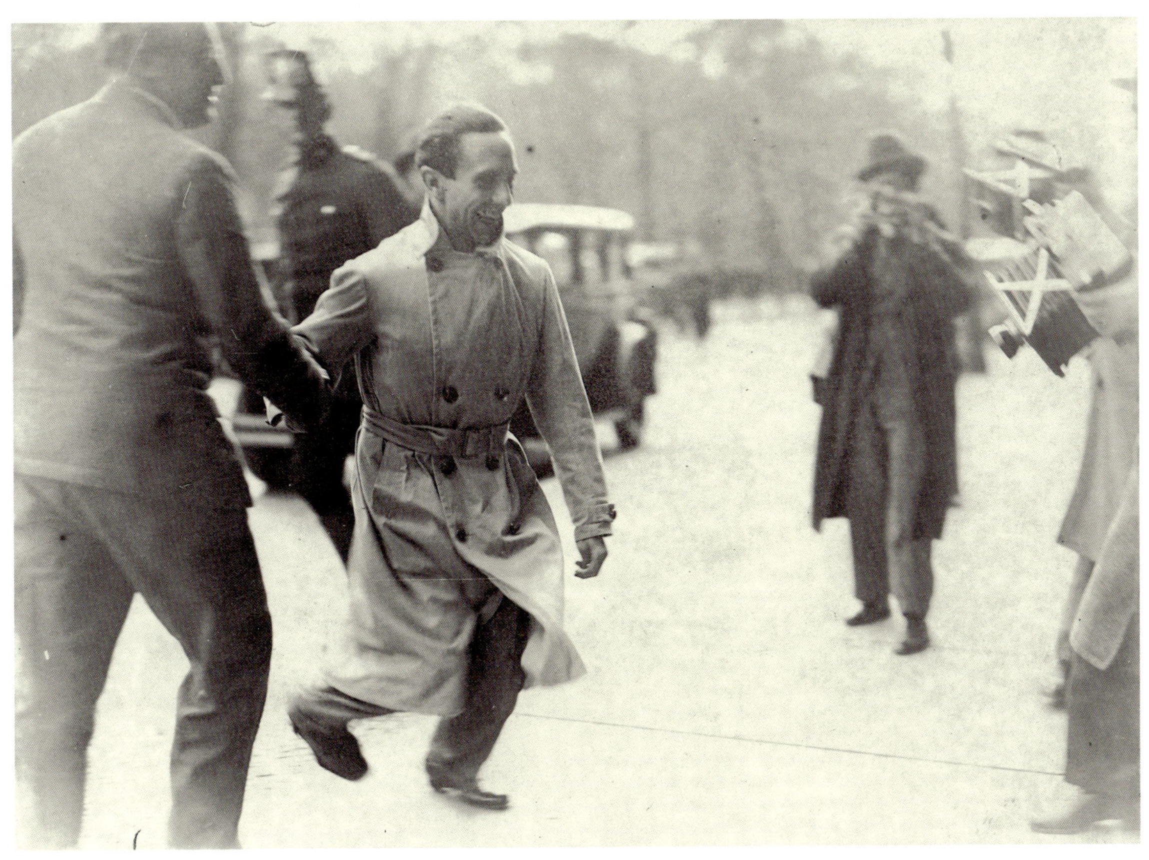

A. Gross, Berlin

The leader of the Nationalist Party, Dr. Goebbels makes a rush to enter the Reichstag, *undated*

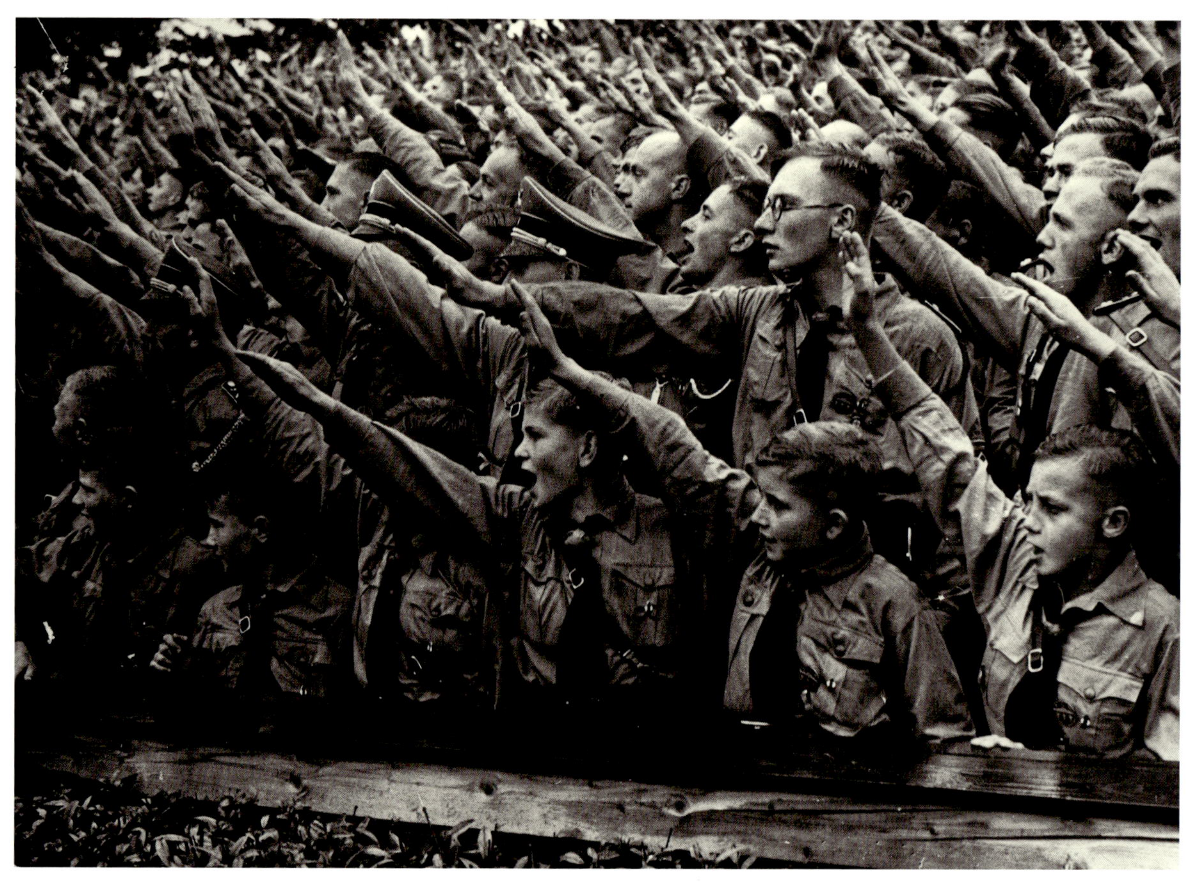

Photographer unknown, Planet News
Nazi Youth Cheers Hitler, *13 September 1937*

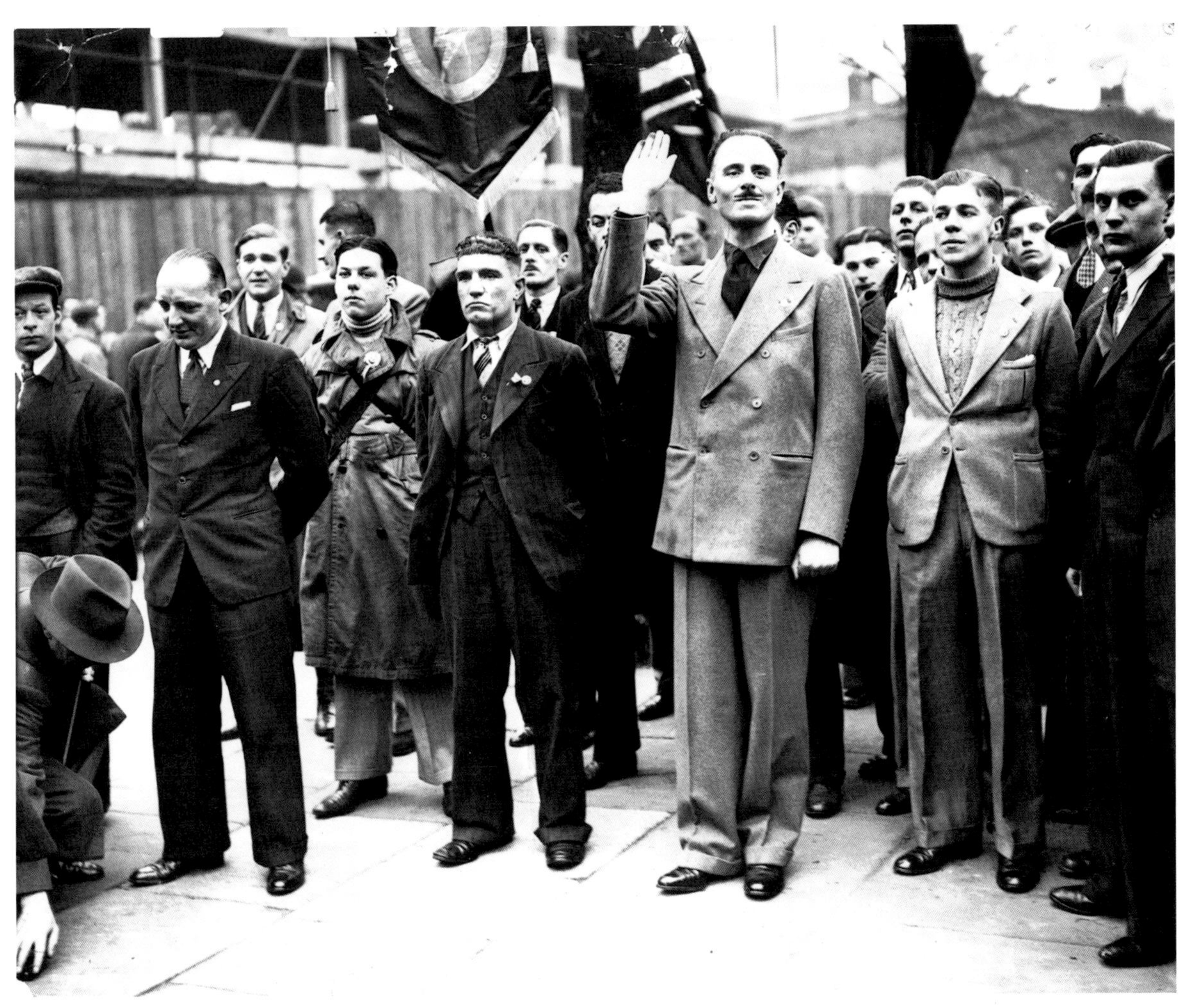

Photographer unknown, Central Press
Sir Oswald Mosley gives a fascist salute during his march to Bermondsey, *1938*

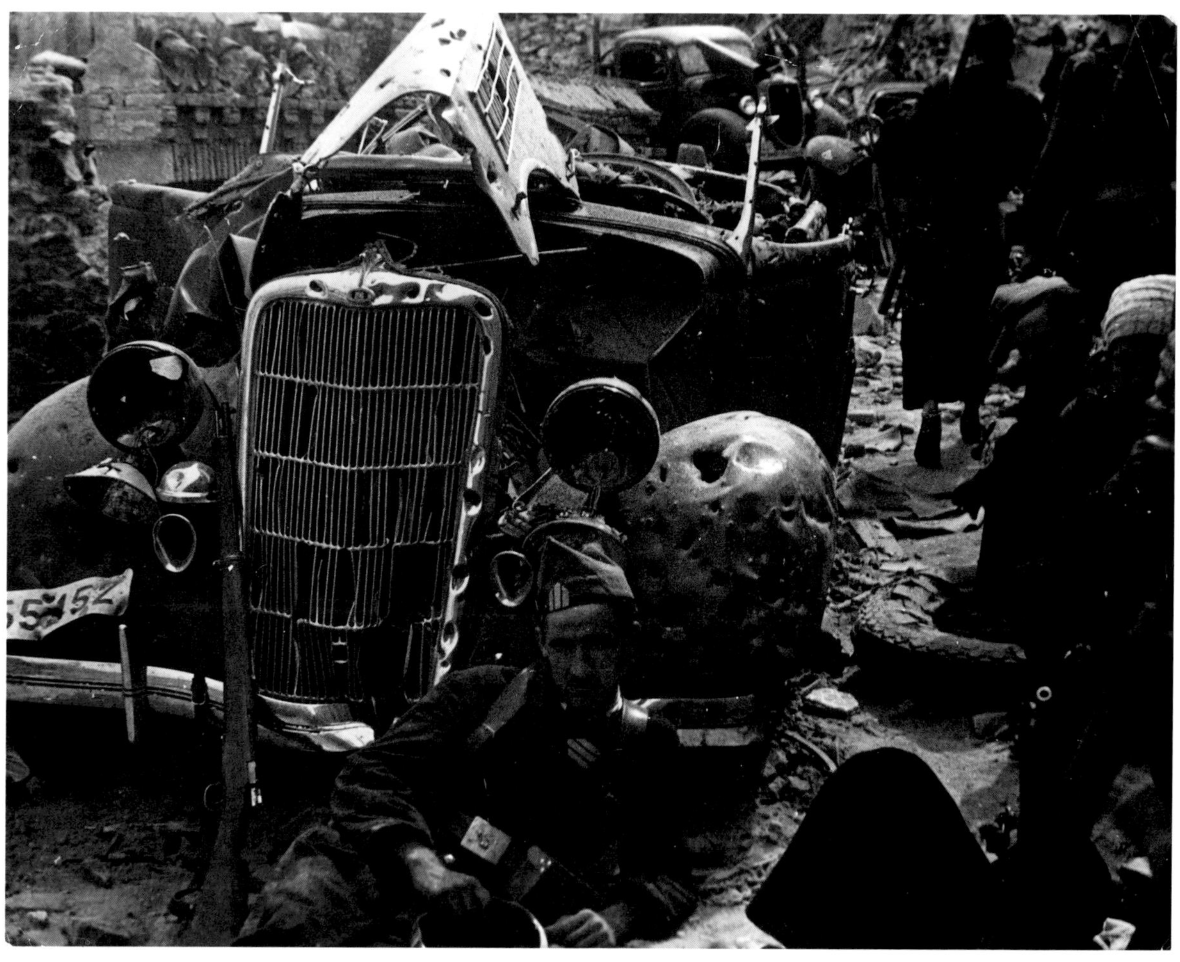

Photographer unknown, Three Lions
Spanish Refugees, *undated*
Scene of destruction along the road leading from the Spain of
Franco to the then still freedom loving France.

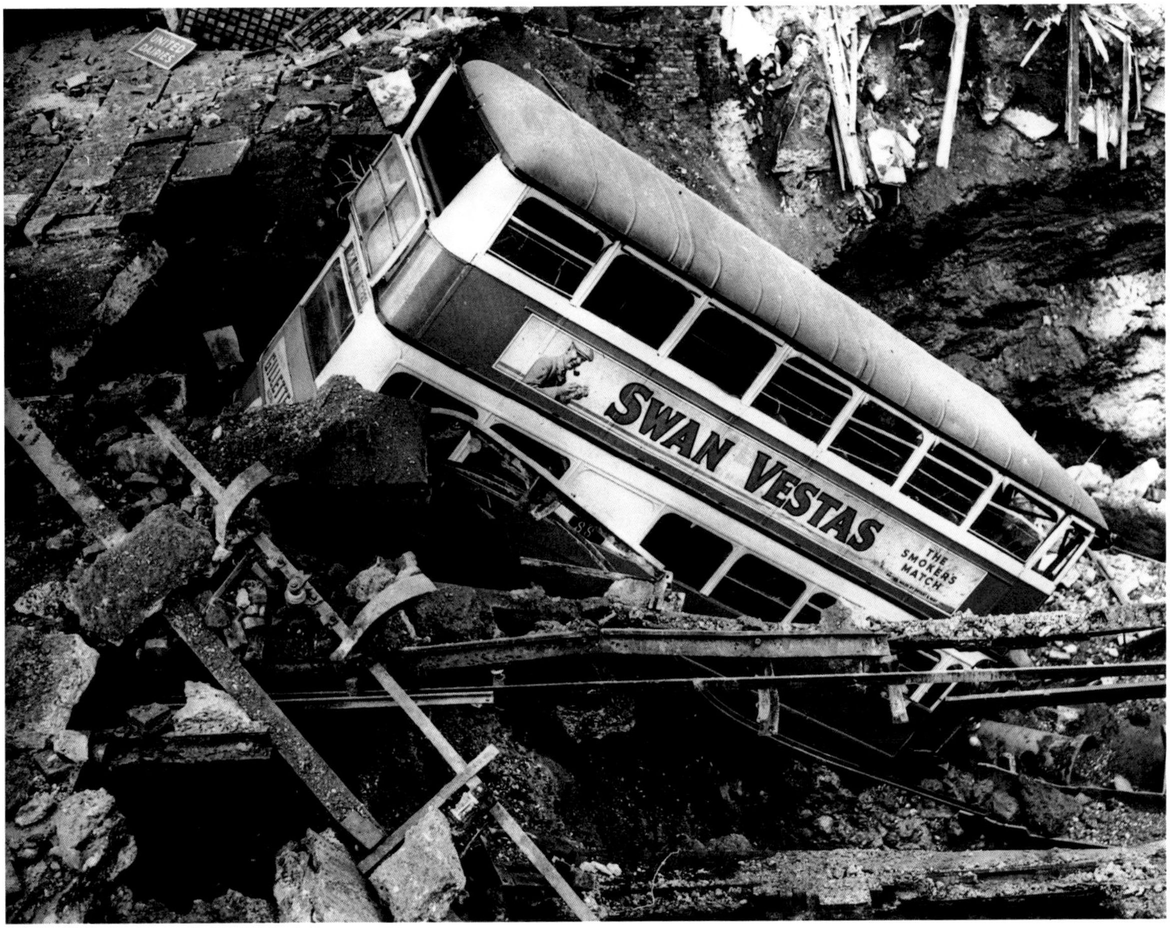

Photographer unknown, Fox Photos
World War II, London Blitz, Balham, *12 October 1940*
(not passed by War Office censor at the time).

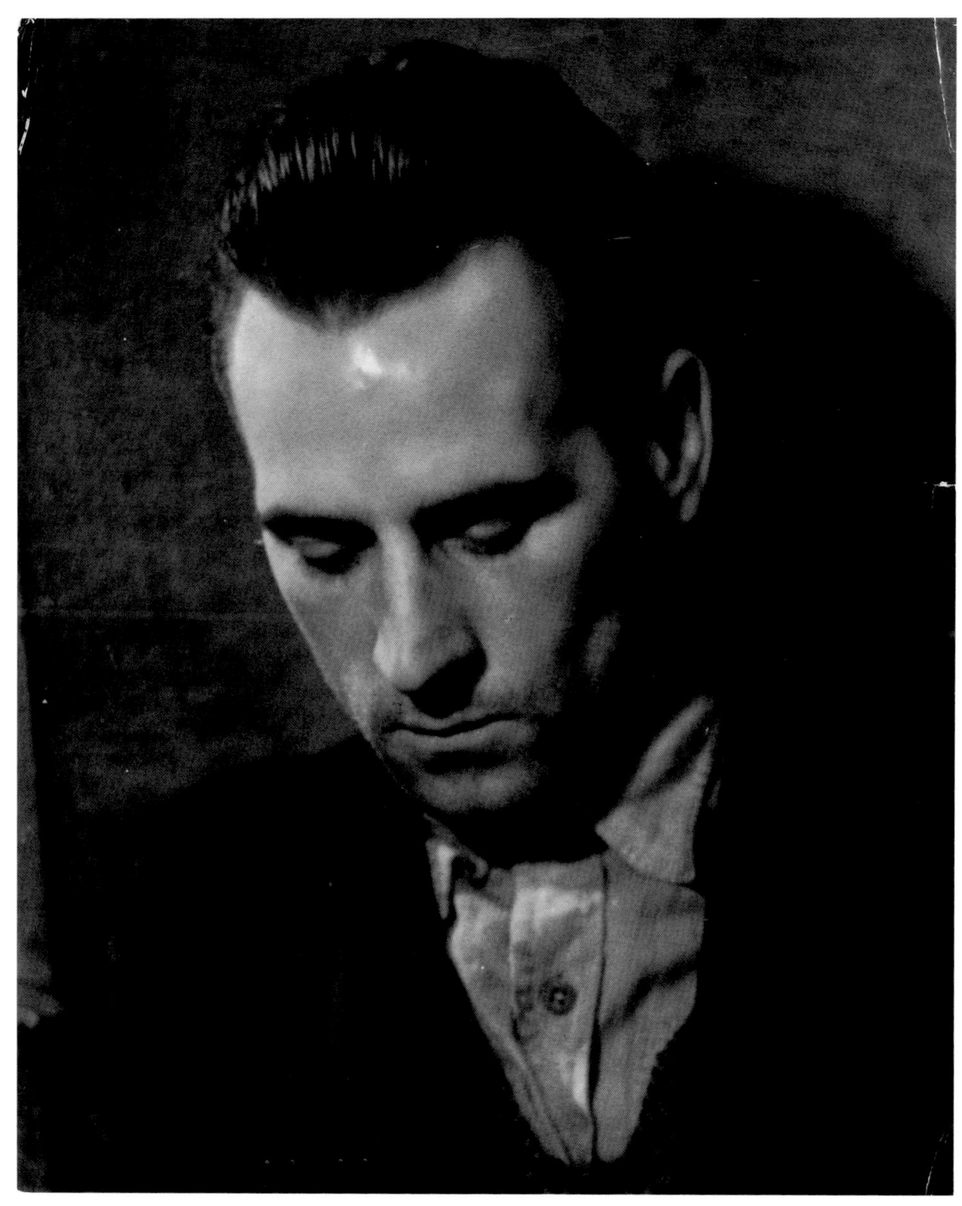

Kurt Hutton
They Had No Work – scenes at the 'Silver Lady's Night Cafe' in Trafalgar Square, *Picture Post, 14 January 1939*

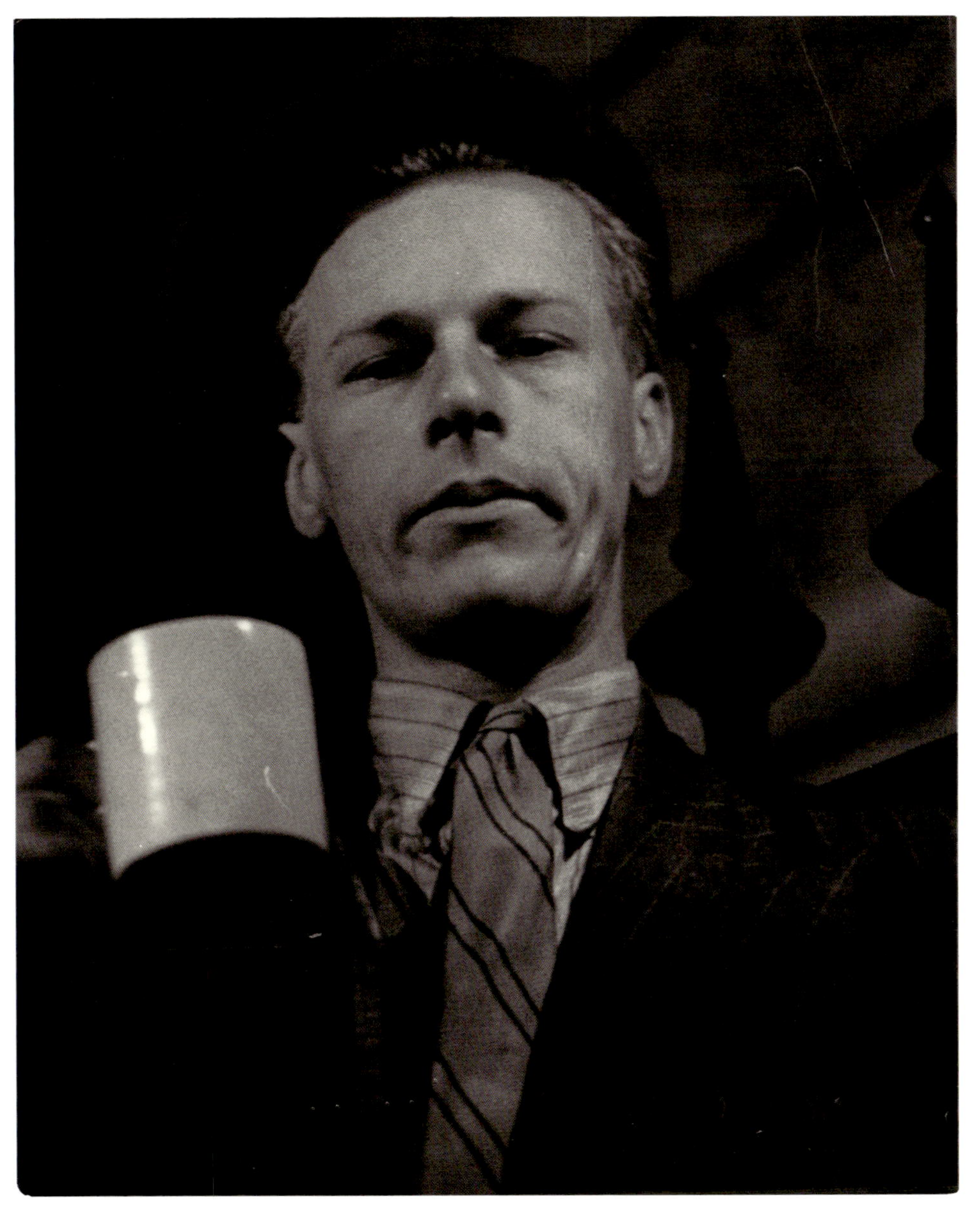

Kurt Hutton
They Had No Work – scenes at the 'Silver Lady's Night Cafe' in Trafalgar Square, *Picture Post, 14 January 1939*

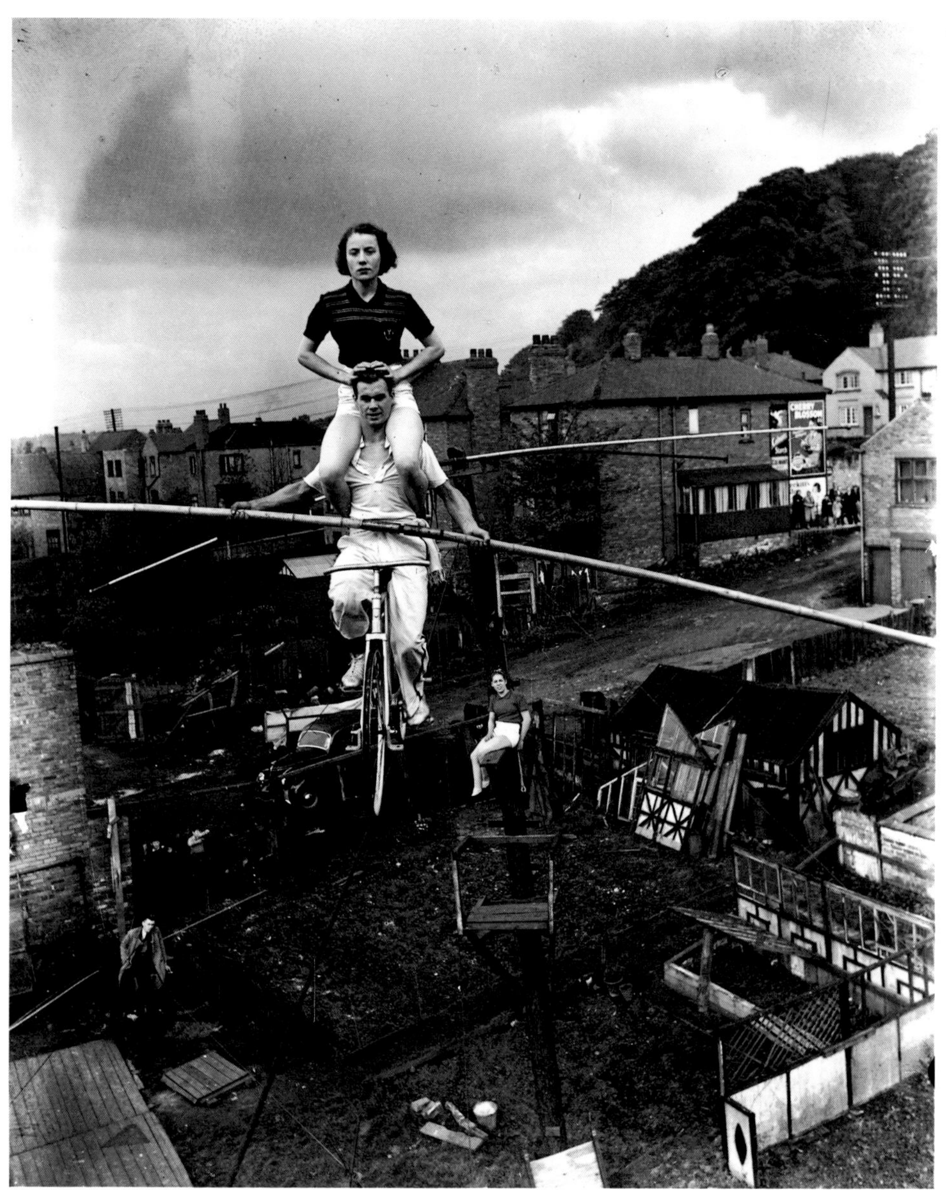

Photographer unknown, Keystone
To Leave Pit for Circus, *23 May 1939*
'The Davis family of Maltby are giving up their jobs at the mine
and taking their wire walking act on the road.'

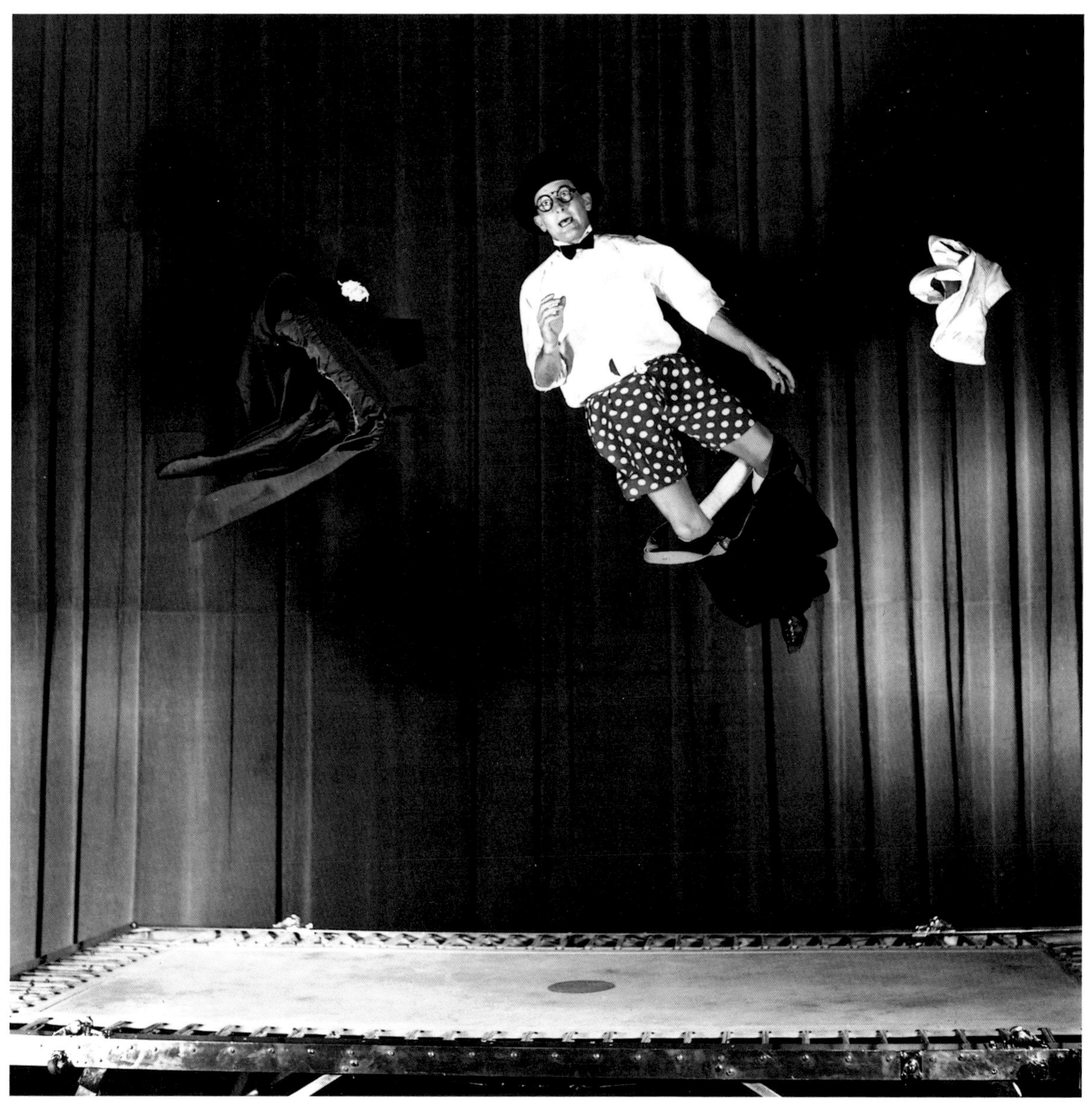

Charles H. Hewitt
High Jinks, *Picture Post, 22 October 1949*
Melvyn, one of the members of the Rudell Acrobatic Trio
performing at the London Palladium.

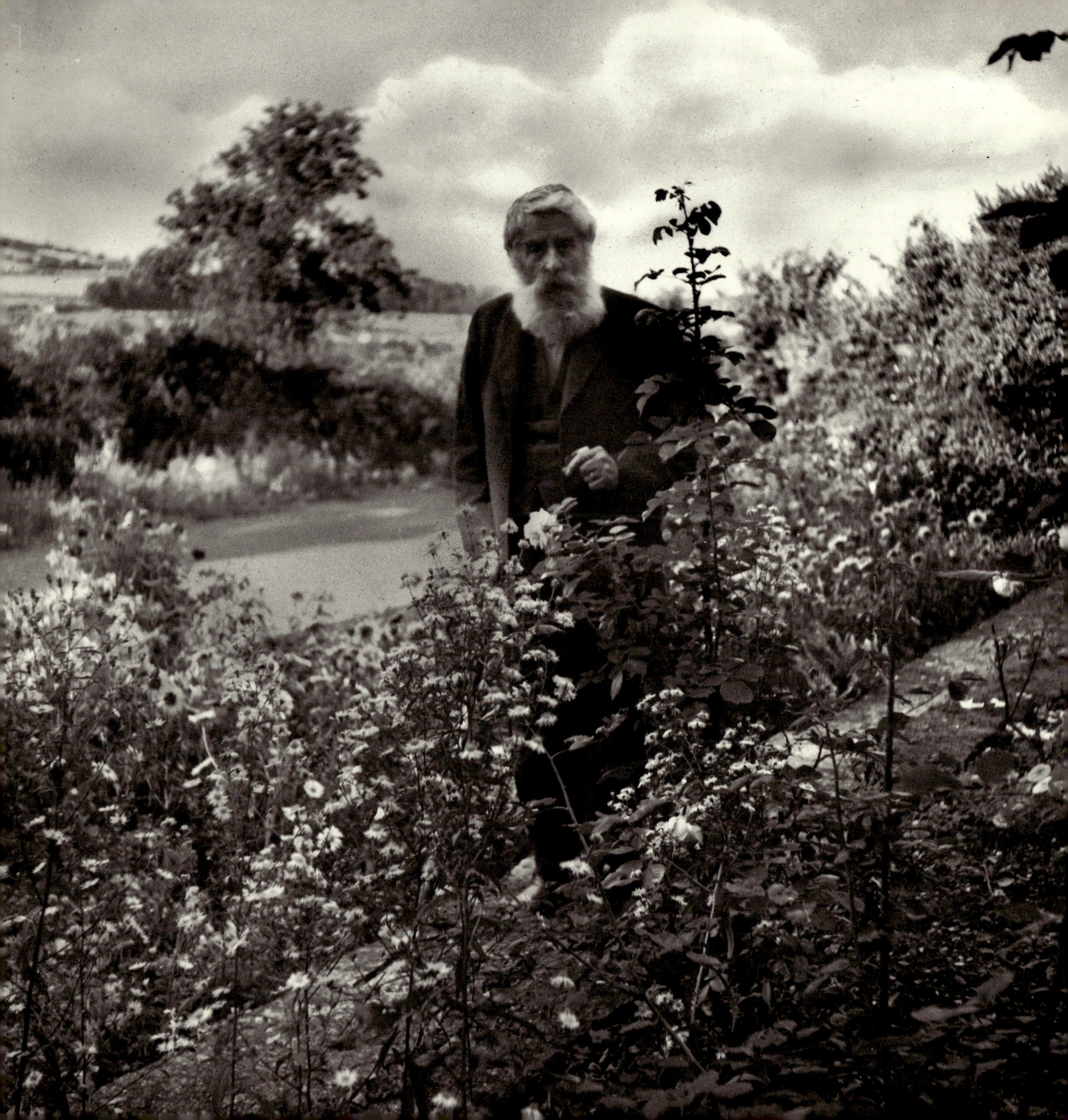

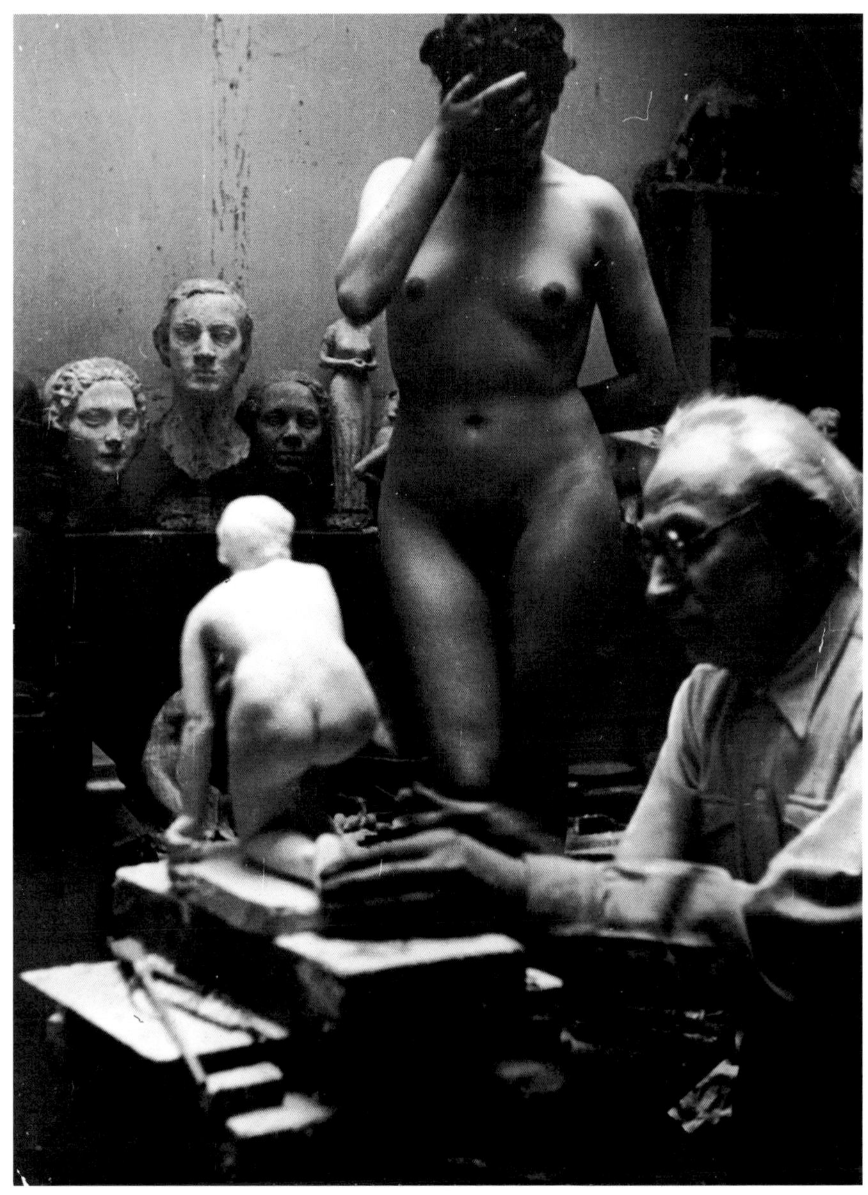

Photographer unknown, Aral Photo, Paris
Artist's Model, *undated*

Cecil Beaton
Walter Sickert in his garden, *1941*

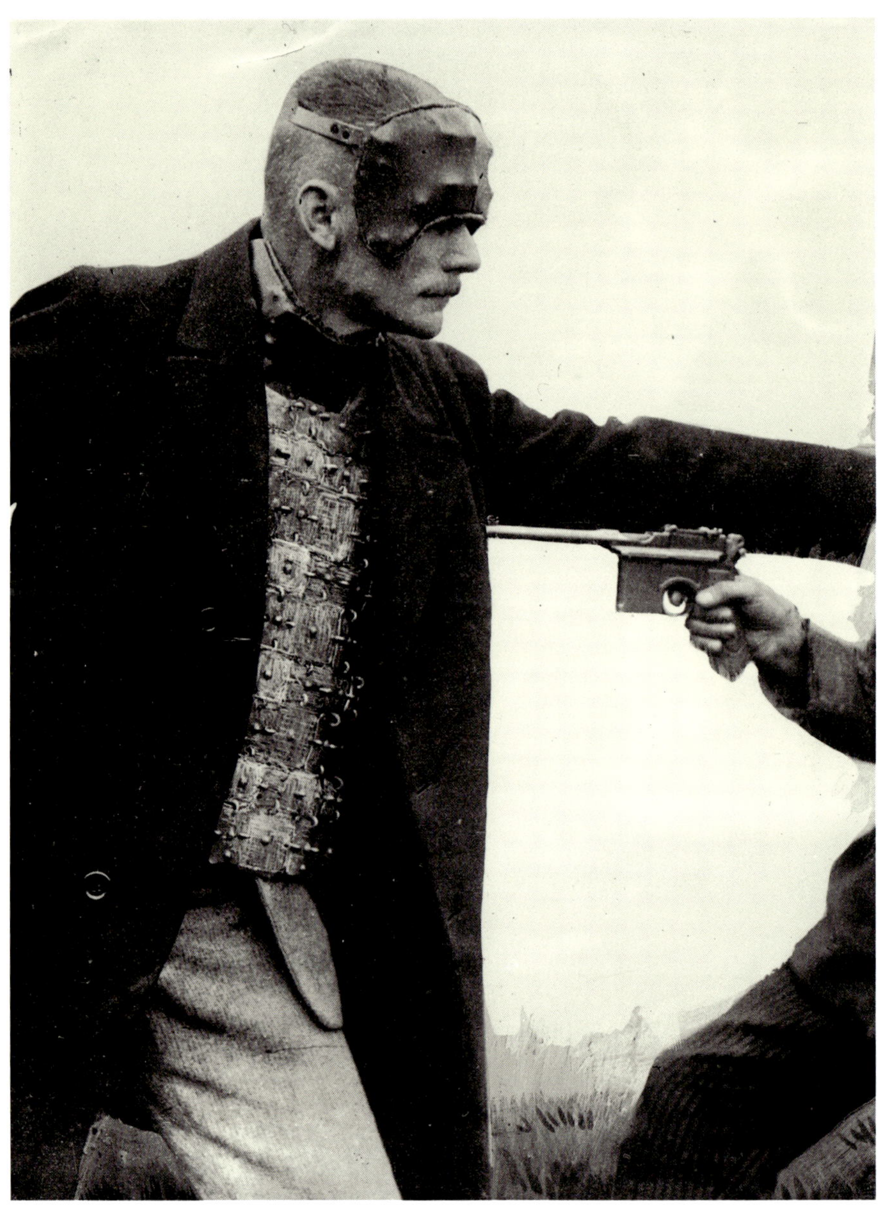

Photographer unknown, G.P.A.
The Armour of Civil Strife, *Germany c1930*
'A breast plate and helmet of alloy as used by the police in
Germany in their pursuit of unscrupulous and desperate criminals.'

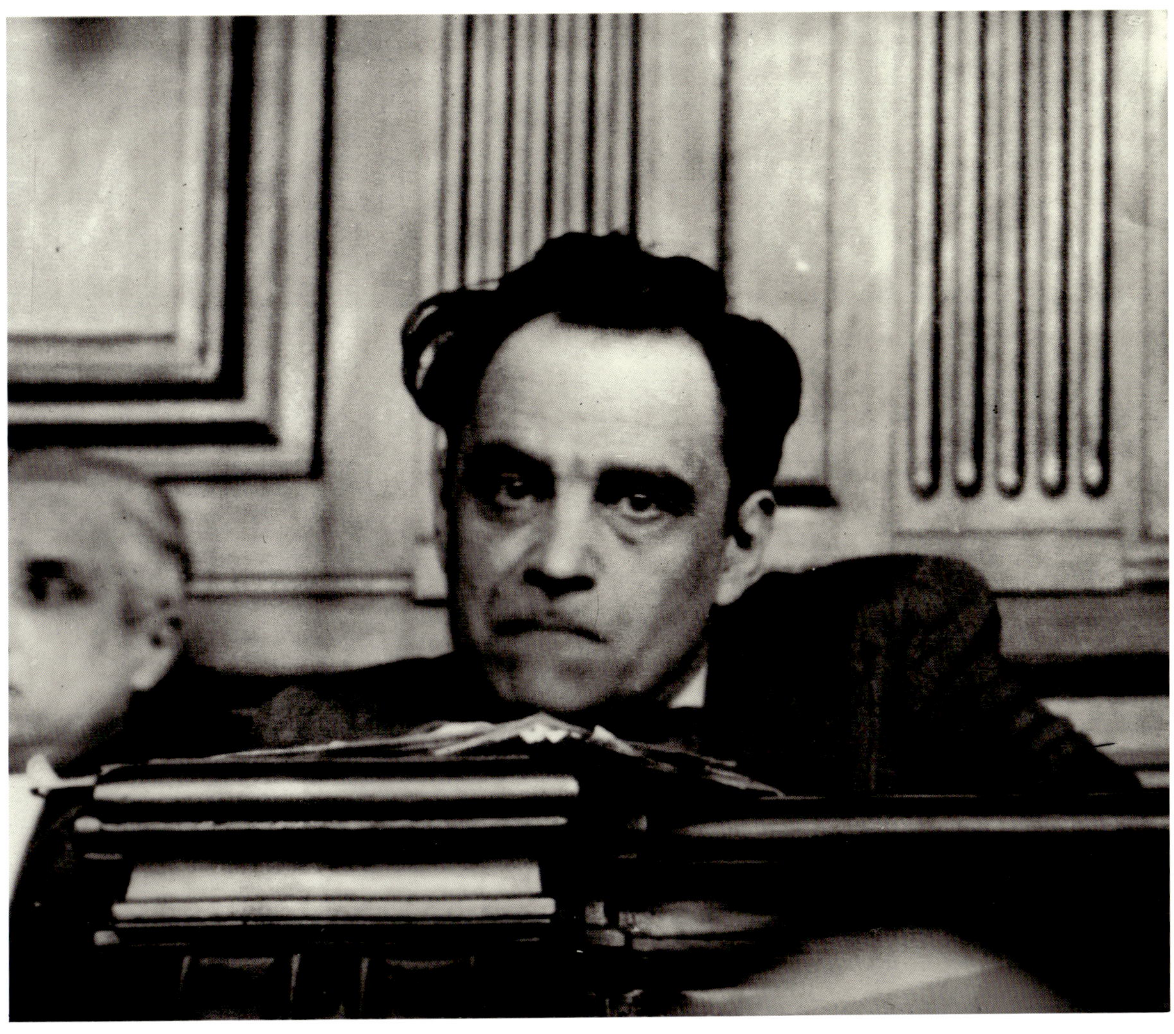

Photographer unknown, Planet News
Mass Murder Trial Opens in Paris, *Picture Post, 19 March 1946*
'In the dock Dr. Marcel Petiot, accused of the murder of 27
persons, betrays rage in his face as he argues with the Public
Prosecutor before the Assize Court in Paris.'

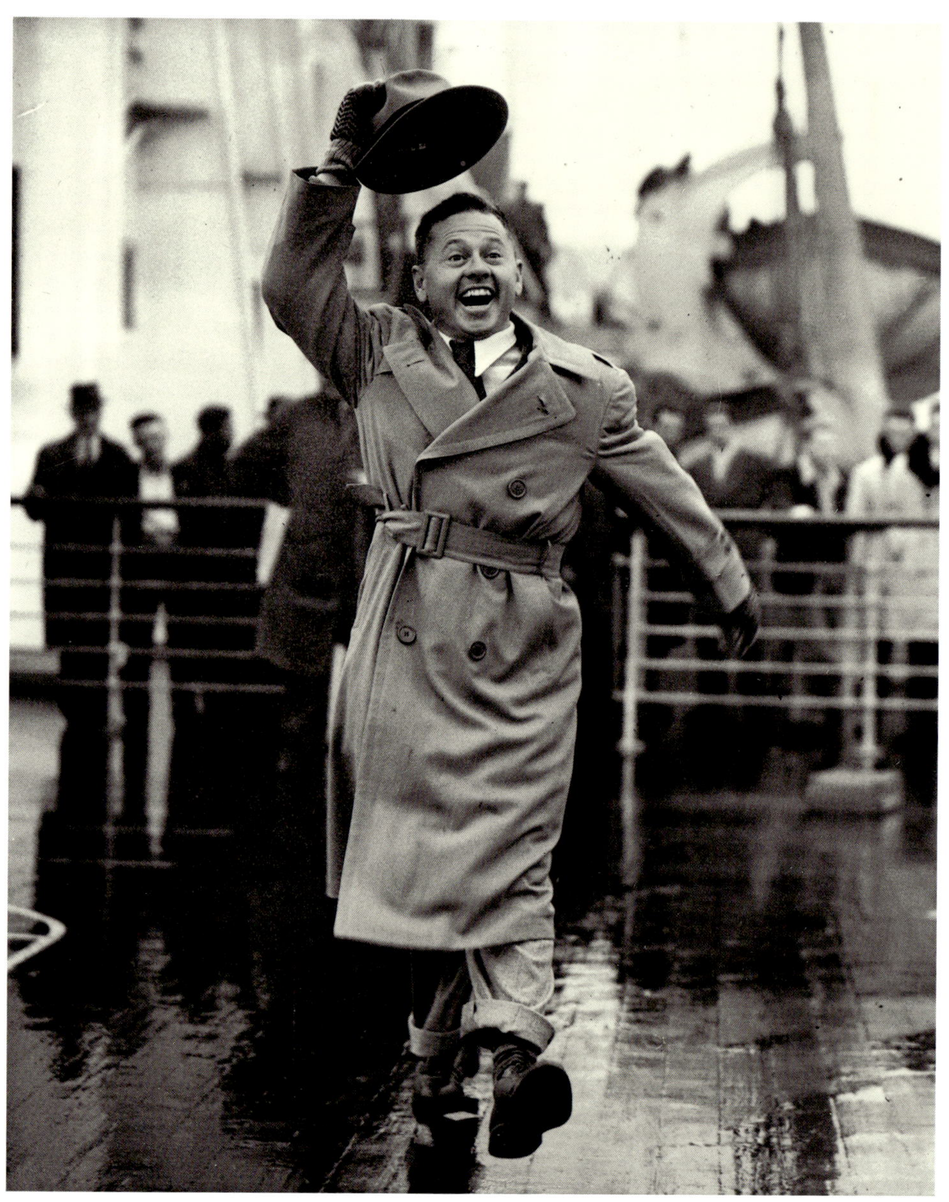

Photographer unknown, P.A. Reuter
'Andy Hardy' steps out, *1 January 1948*
'Screen actor Mickey Rooney, famous for his Andy Hardy roles,
steps out briskly, as he arrives at Southampton from New York.'

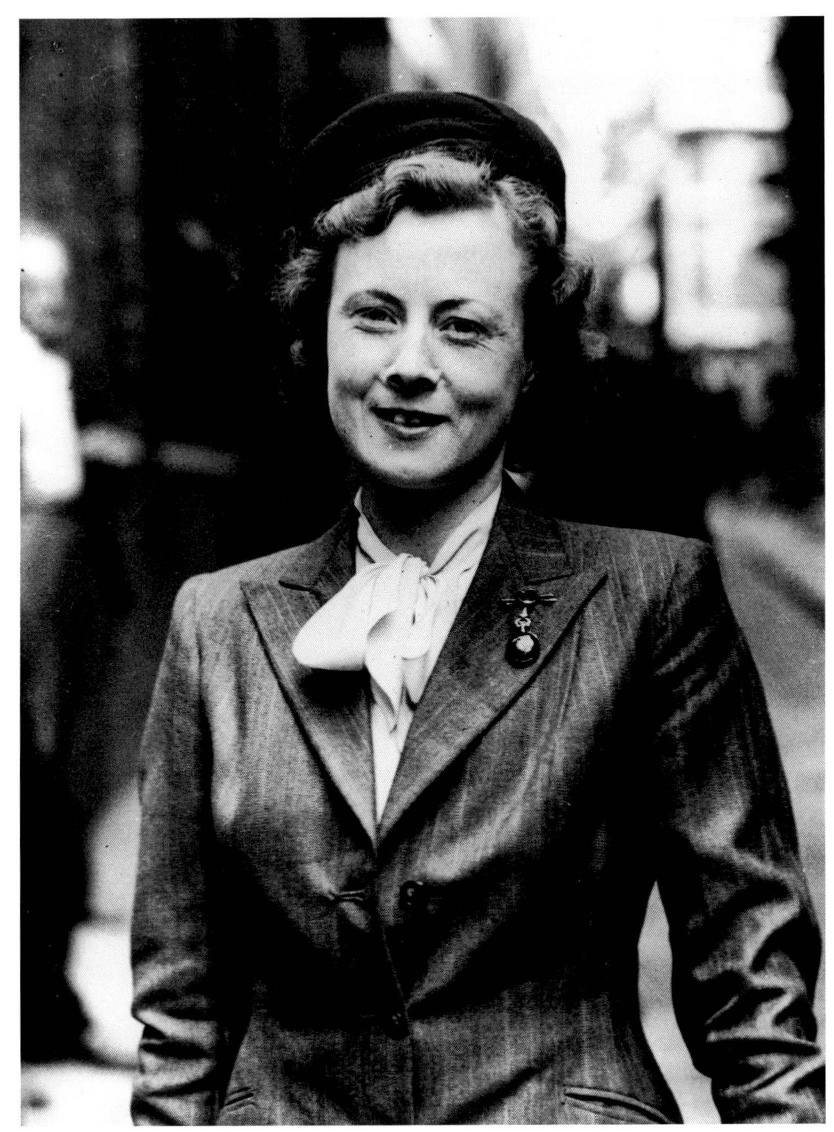

Photographer unknown
Barbara Castle, *c1950*

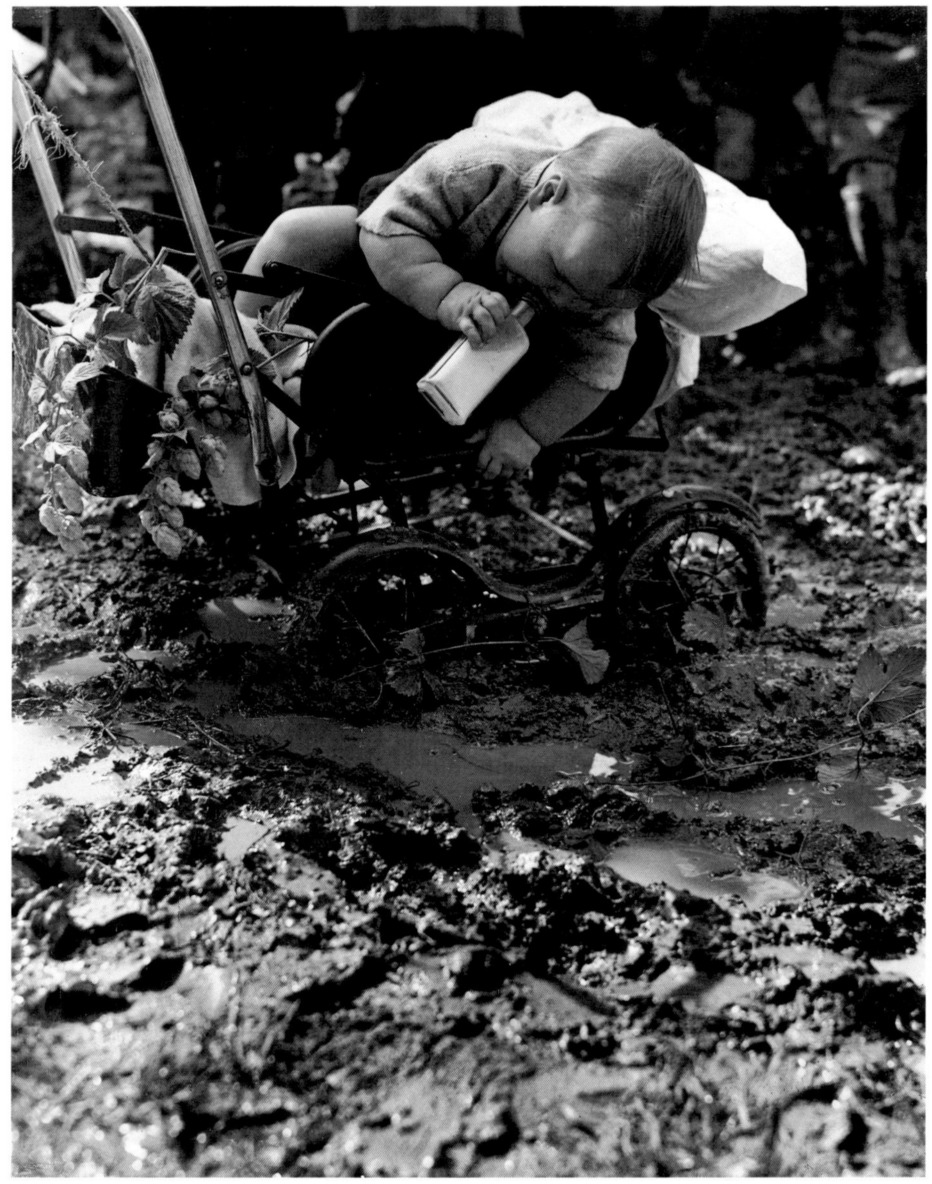

Photographer unknown, Keystone
'He prefers his milk to beer any day – even in the hopfields . . .',
6 September 1946

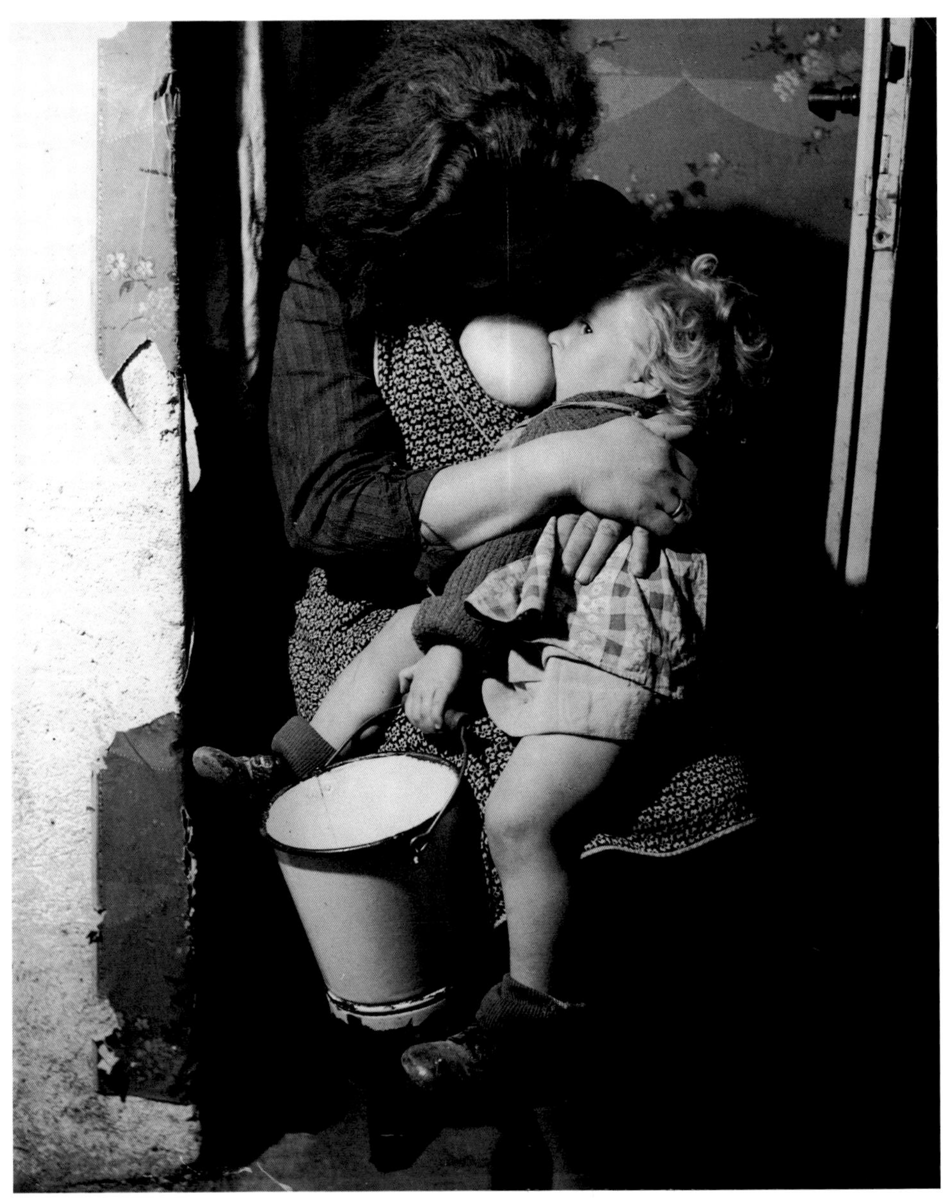

Werner Bischof
Europe's Children, *Picture Post, 24 April 1948*
Issue of *Picture Post* devoted to the plight of children in war torn Europe.

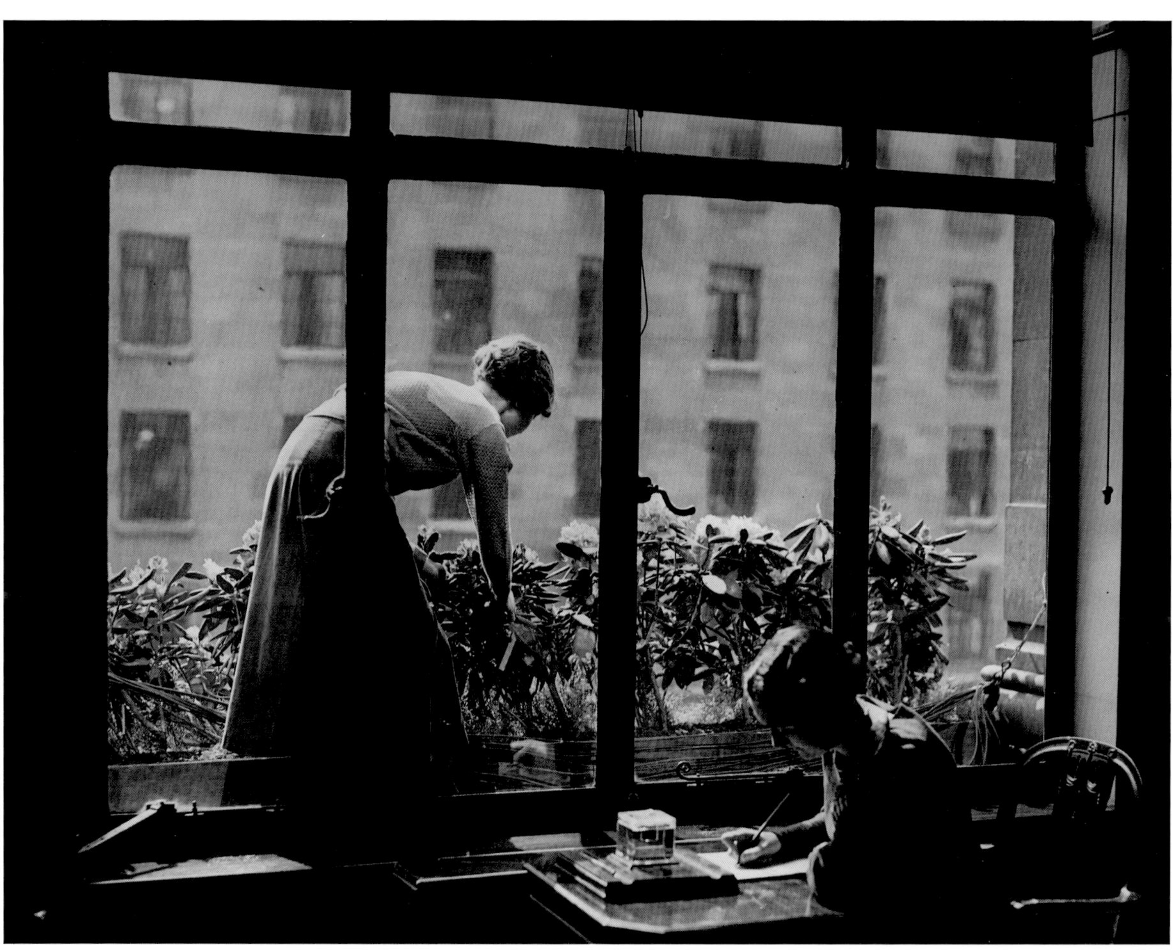

Photographer unknown, Fox Photos
Office Window Box, *1930s*

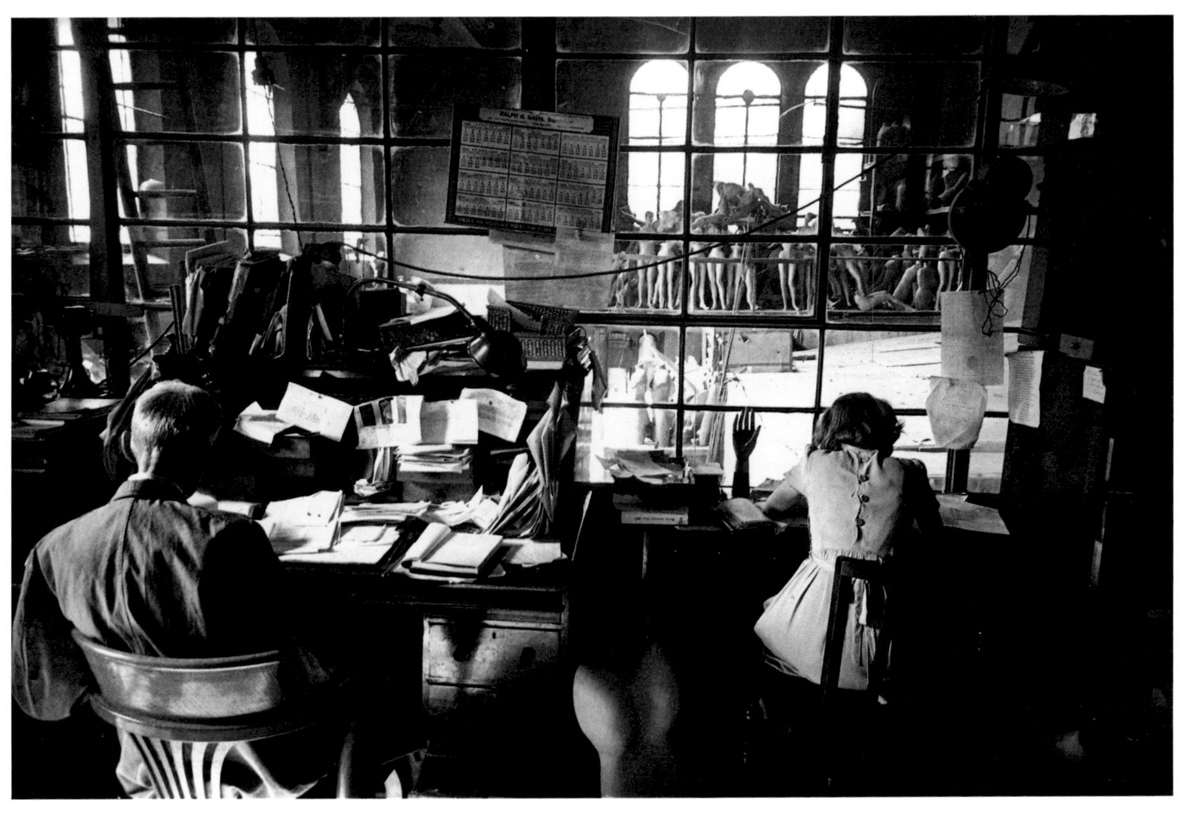

Kurt Hutton
Have You a Good Figure?, *Picture Post, 25 November 1950*
The strange factory of Gems Ltd. who made wax and composition
models in a chapel off the Portobello Road.

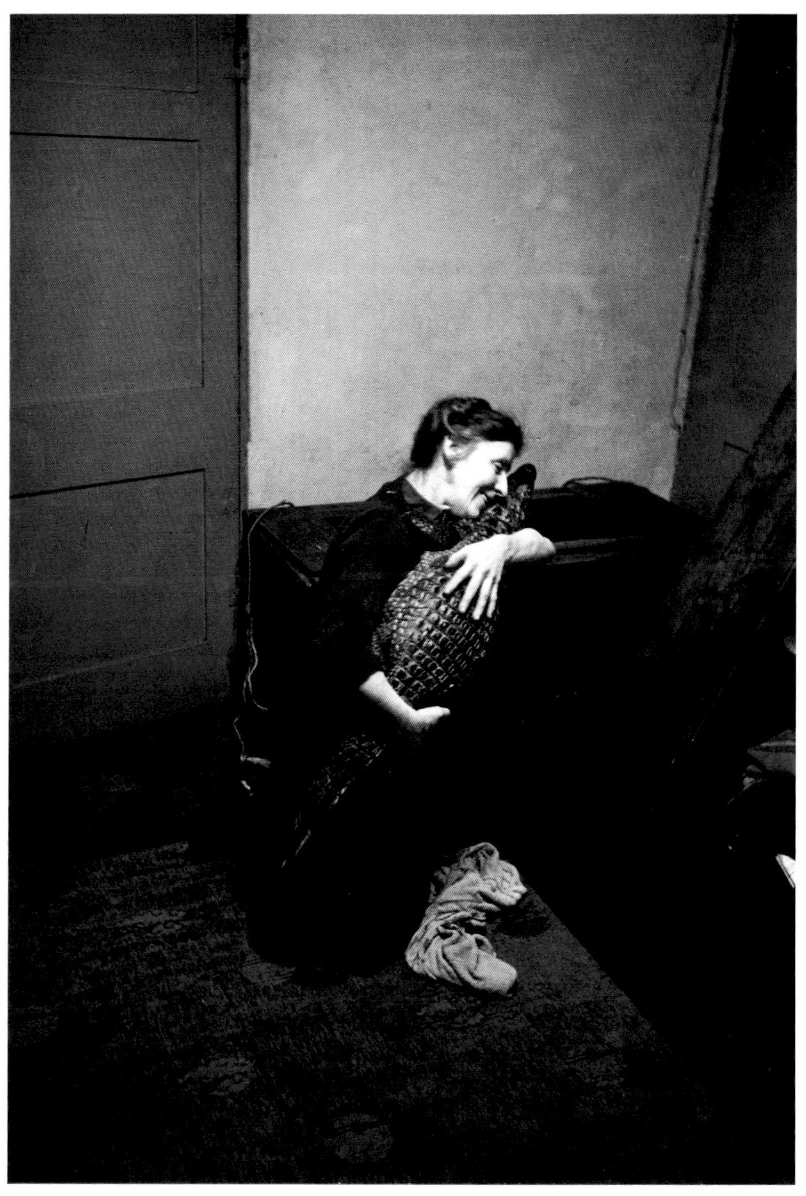

Charles H. Hewitt
Alligators and Old Lace, *Picture Post, 10 January 1948*
'Miss Enid Davis with ''Peter'' a 22 year old female alligator from
Madagascar.'

Bert Hardy
Chelsea Party, *1952 (killed story)*

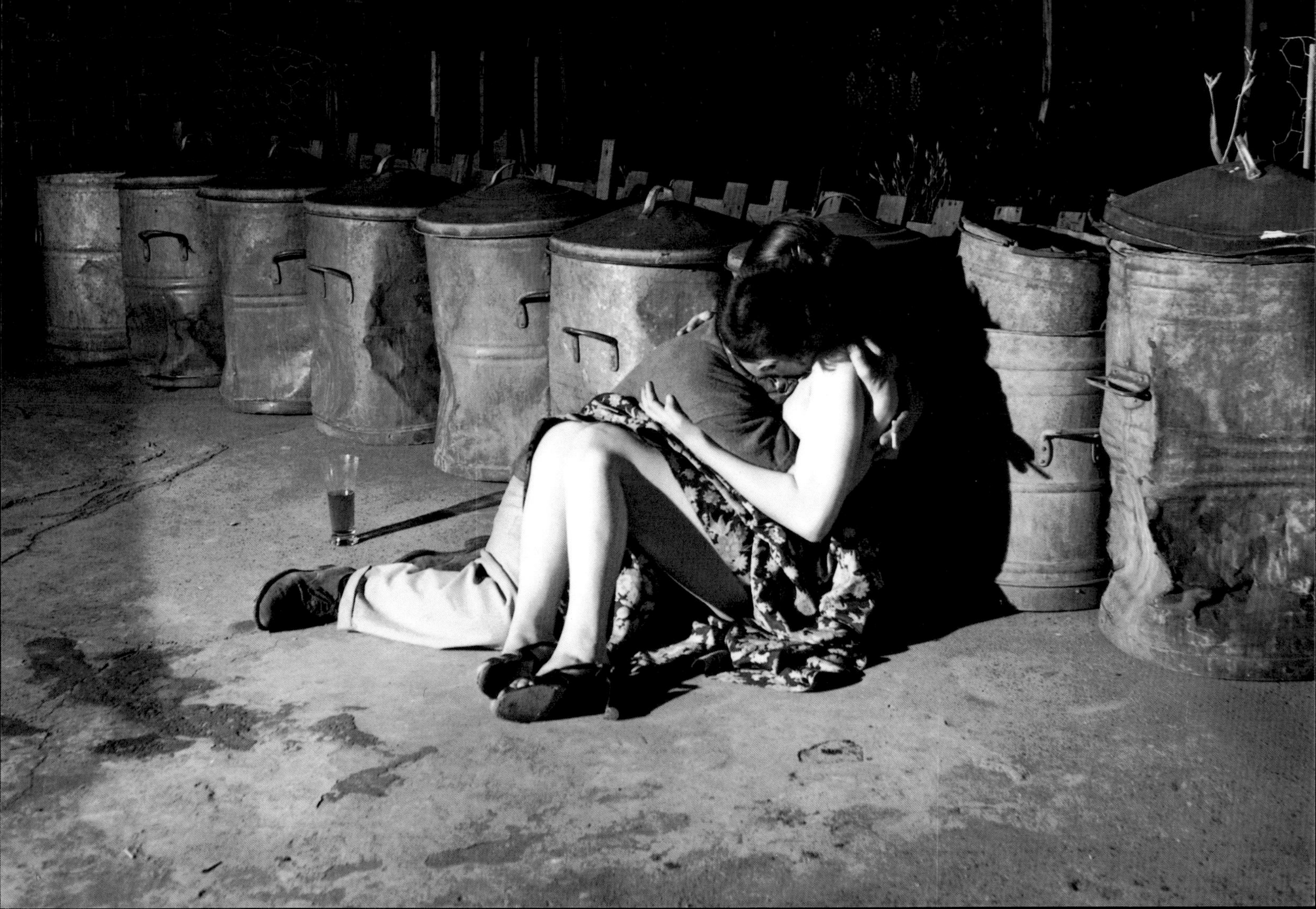

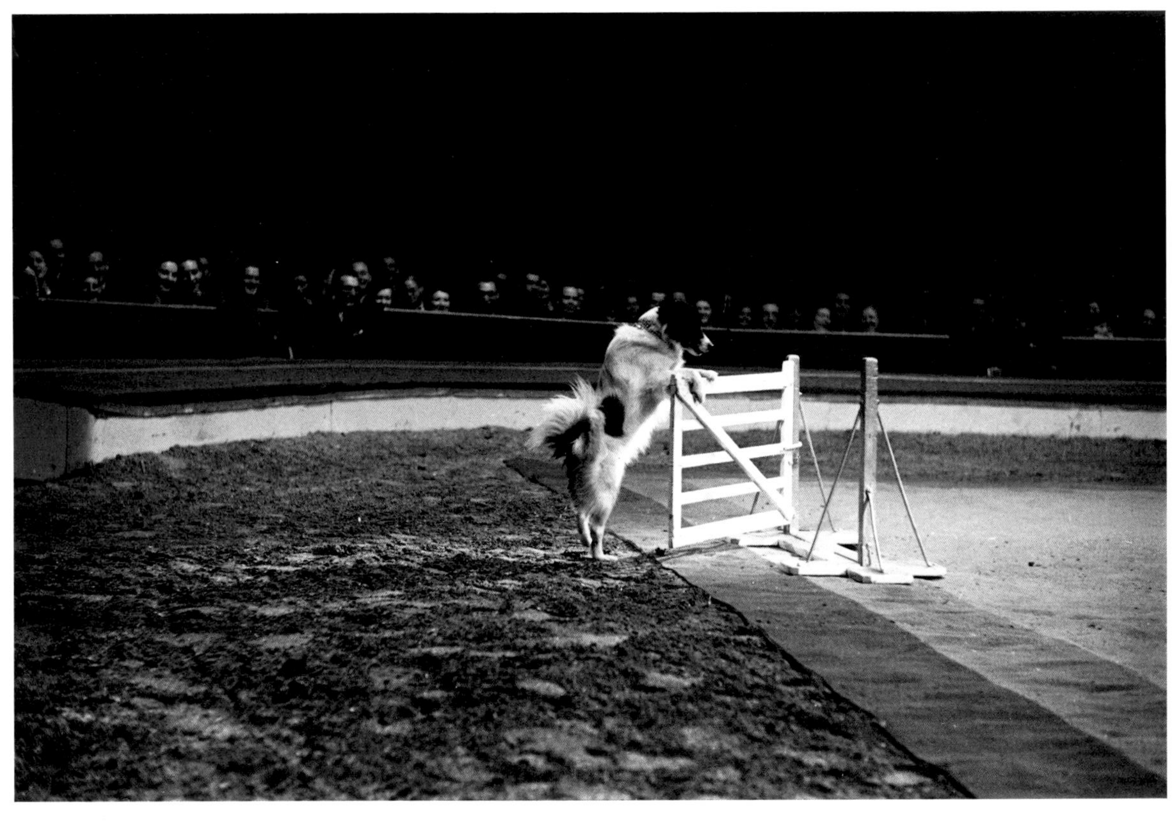

Kurt Hutton
The Circus Again, *Picture Post, 11 January 1947*
'After seven blacked-out years Bertram Mills circus returns to Olympia.'

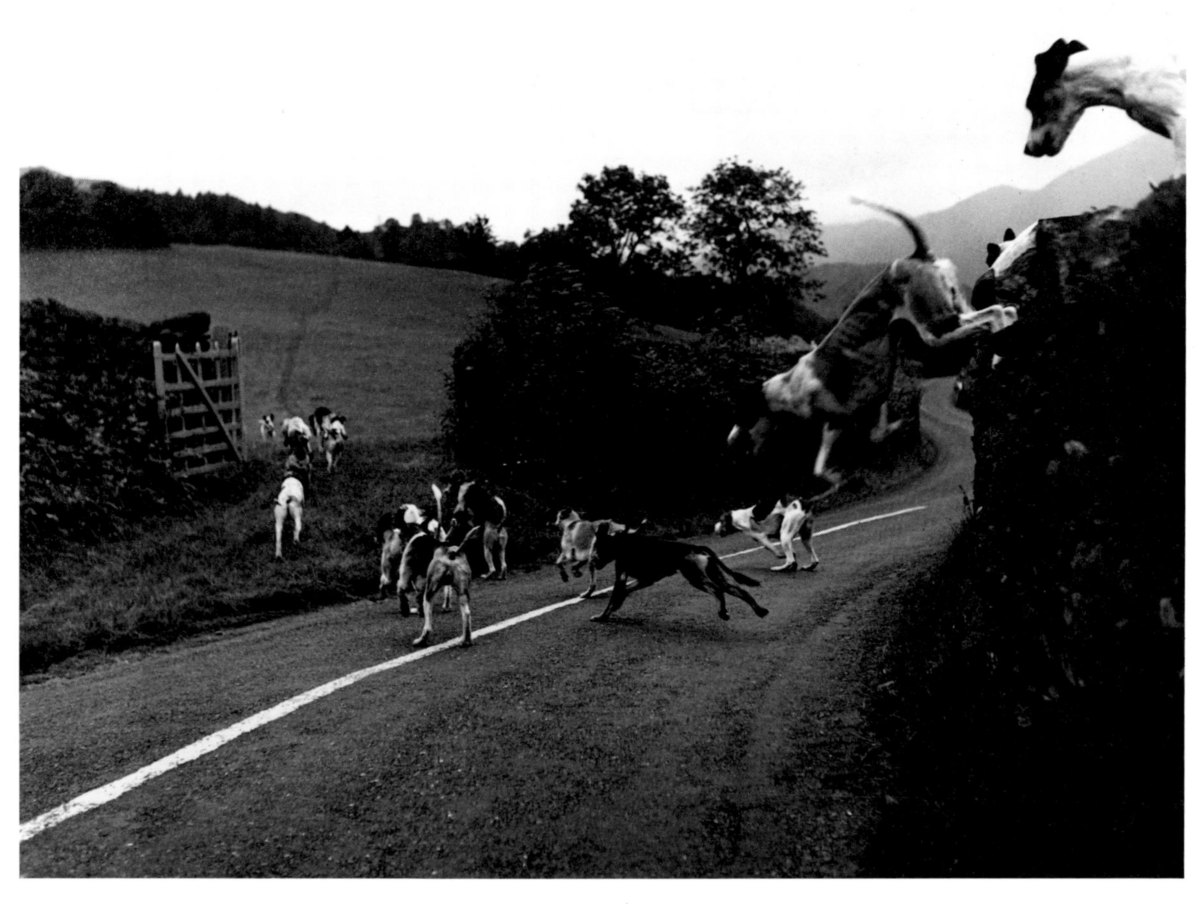

Daniel Farson
Hound Trailing, *Picture Post, 8 September 1951*

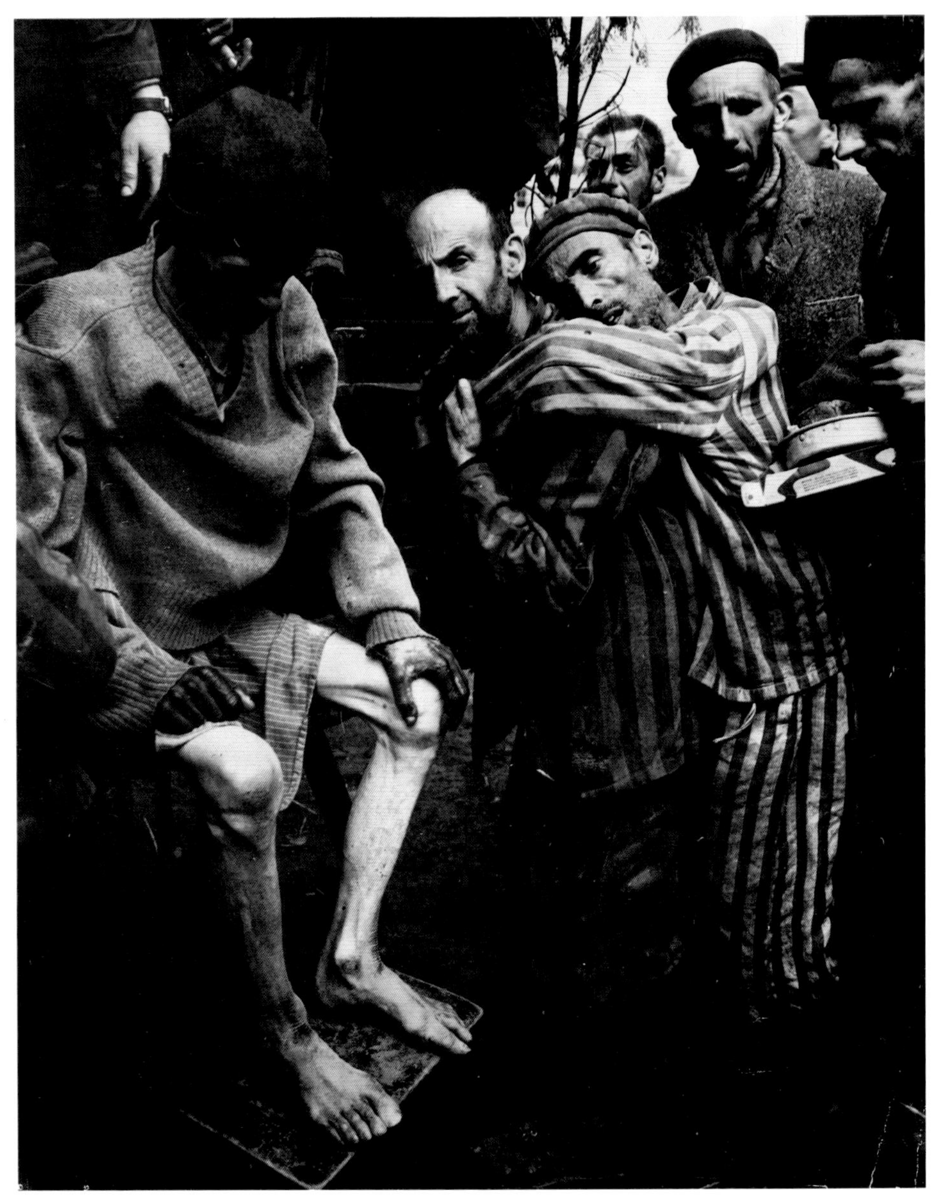

Private Ralph Forney, US Army Signal Corps
New Nazi horror camp discovered at Wobbelin, *16 May 1945*

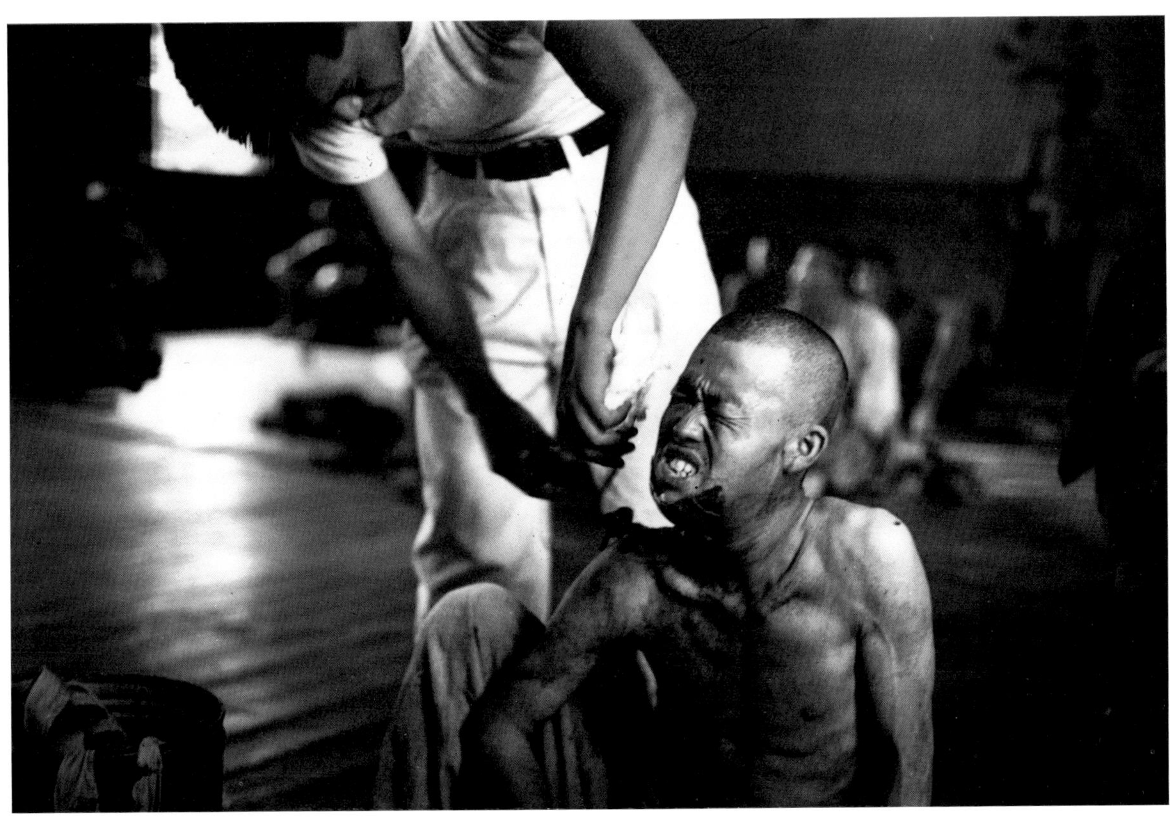

Bert Hardy
War in Korea, *Picture Post, 16 September 1950 (unpublished)*
A North Korean taken prisoner whilst in action near Taegu.

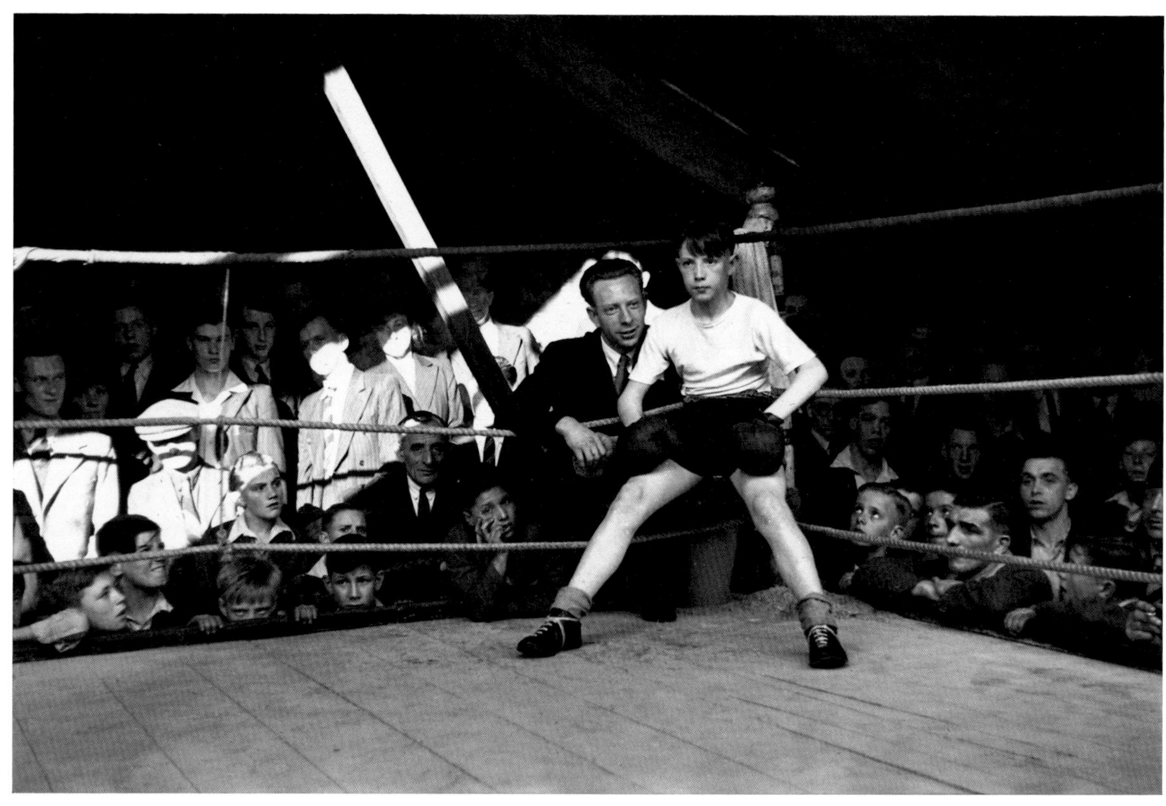

Francis Reiss
Where Champions are Born, *Picture Post, 21 July 1945*
(unpublished)
Hughes of London's boxing pavilion at a Lancashire Fair.

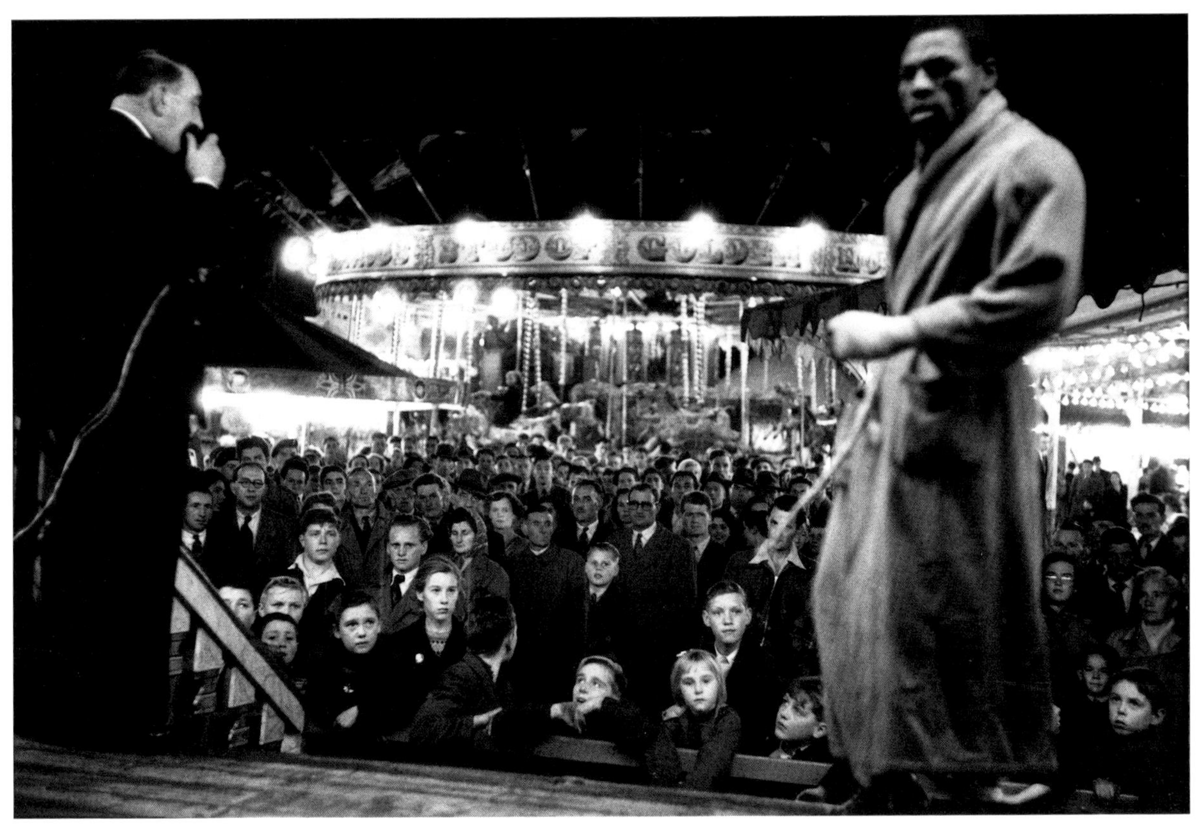

Charles H. Hewitt
'Picture Post' Visits a Fairground Boxing Booth,
Picture Post, 9 January 1954
'Alf Weston's Boxing Academy at a Newbury Fair – the men of
Newbury are not anxious to take on Santos Martin.'

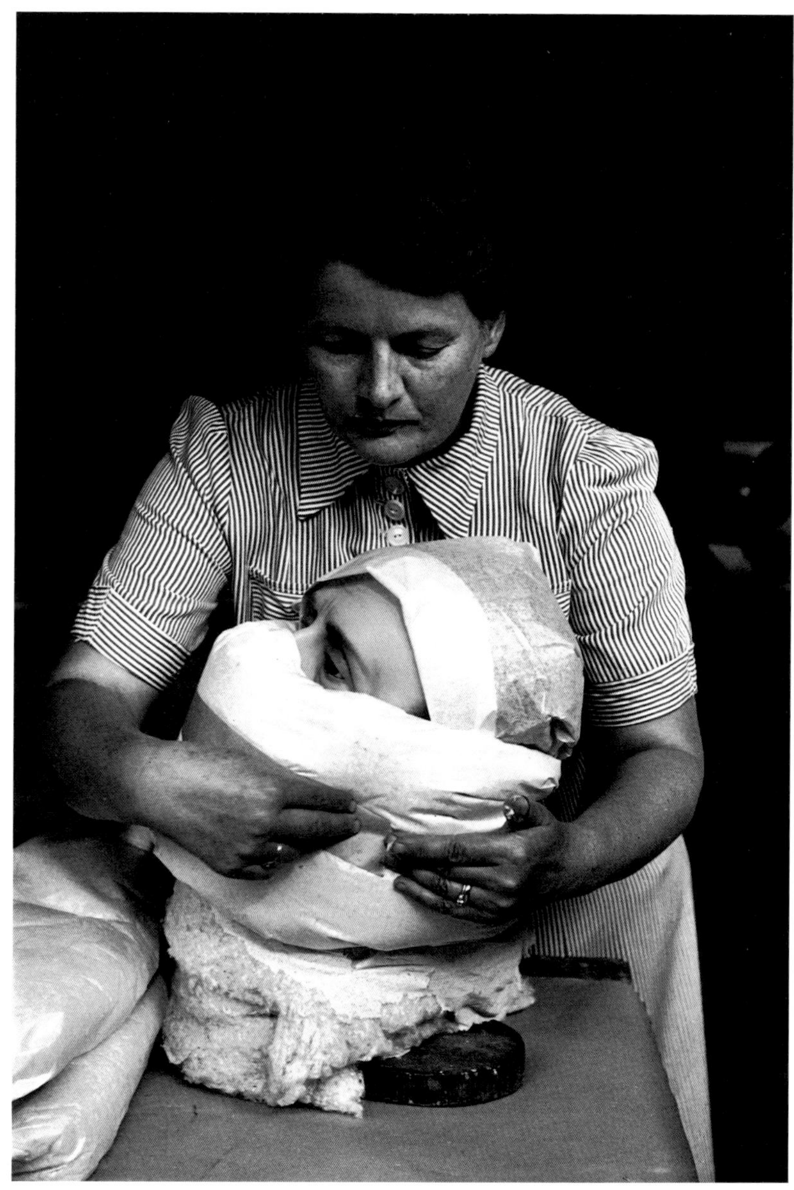

Kurt Hutton
Have You a Good Figure?, *Picture Post, 25 November 1950*
The strange factory of Gems Ltd. who made wax and composition
models in a chapel off the Portobello Road.

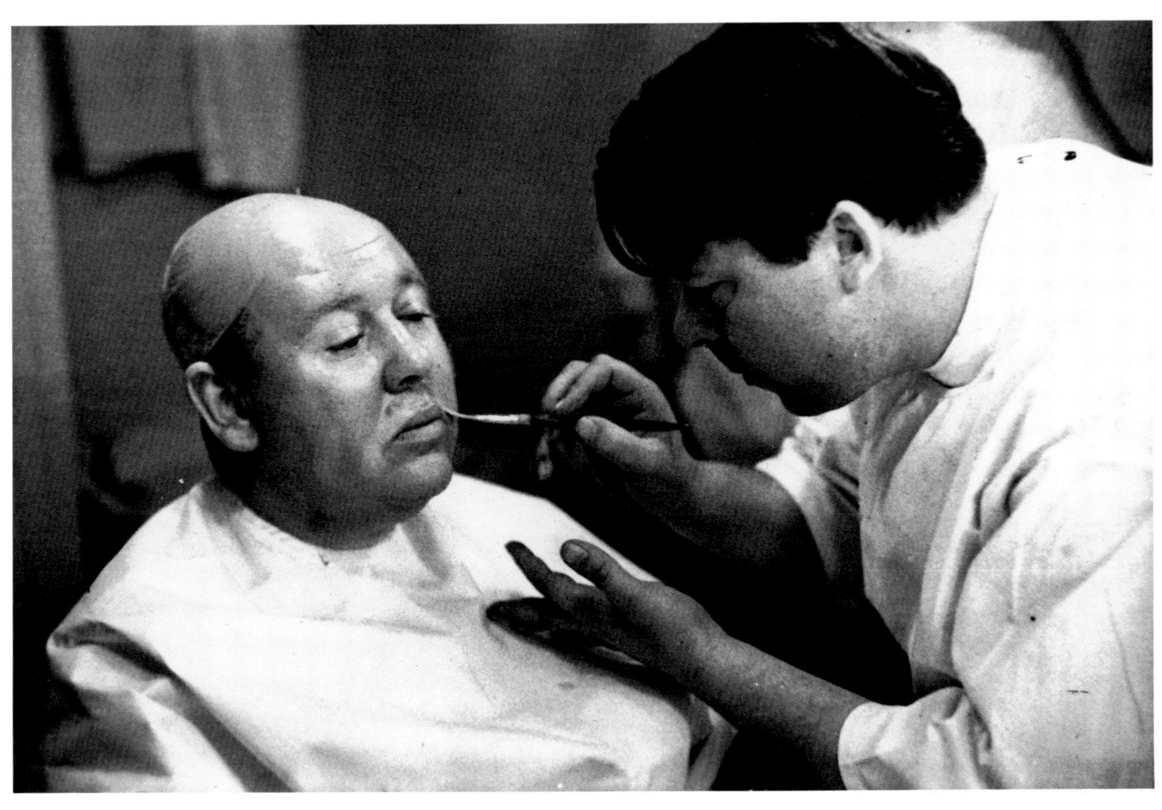

Kurt Hutton
Charles Laughton Makes Up, *24 December 1938*
Charles Laughton being made up for his part as an eighteenth
century squire in the film *Jamaica Inn*.

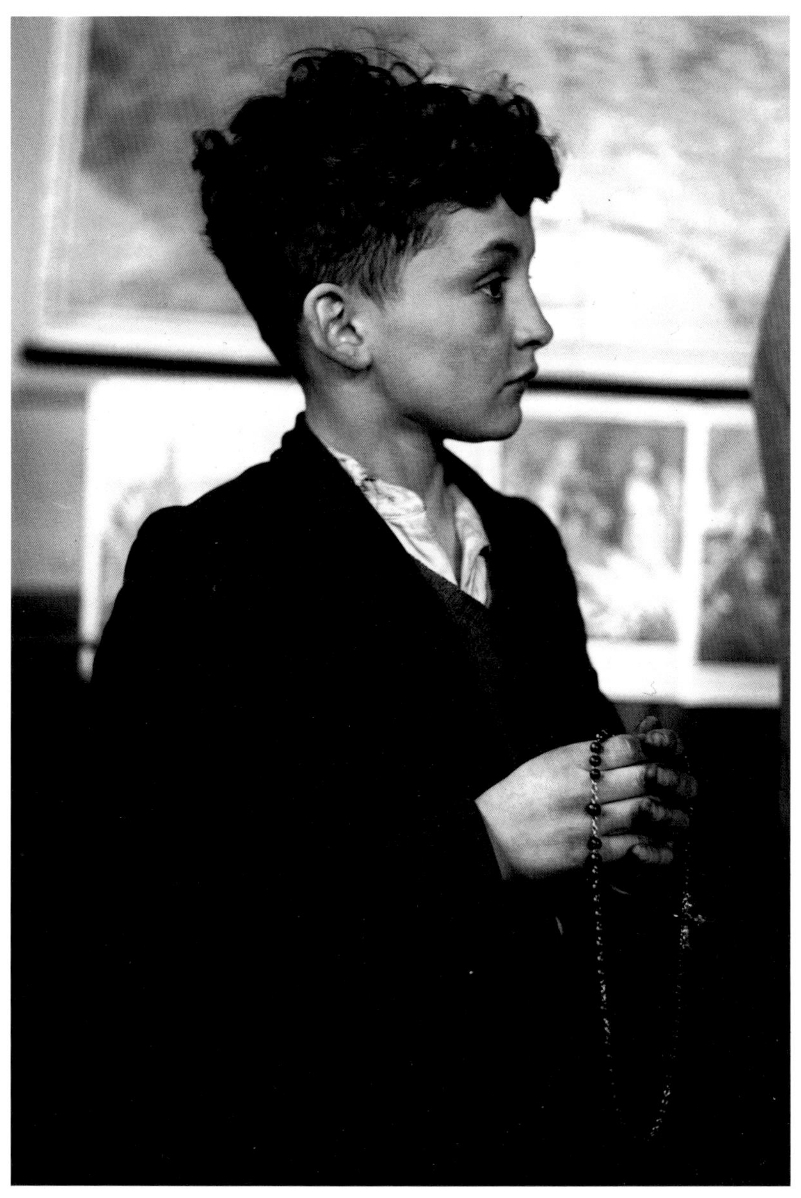

Charles H. Hewitt
Crusader for Prayer, *Picture Post, 26 July 1952 (unpublished)*
Father Patrick Peyton's crusade to restore family prayer to
English homes. A scene in a Durham mining village as the daily
rosary takes place.

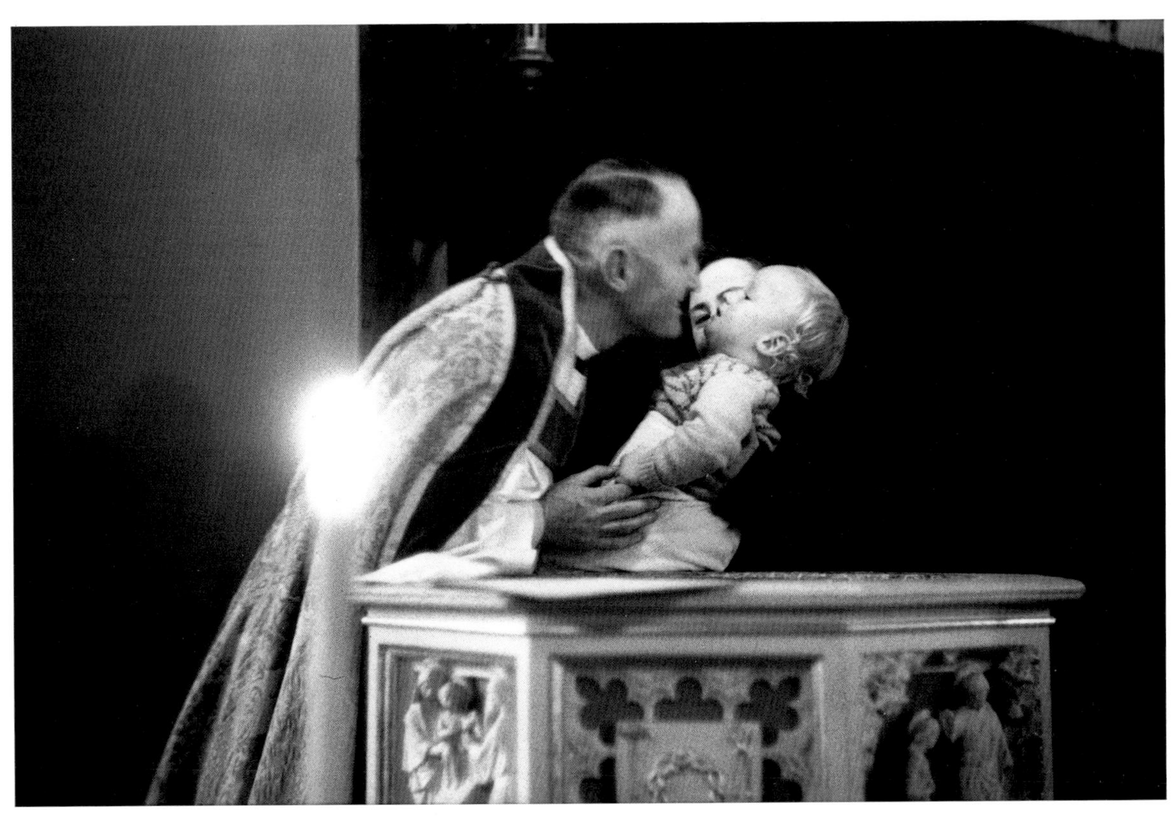

Thurston Hopkins
A Man of Goodwill, *Picture Post, 25 December 1954 (unpublished)*

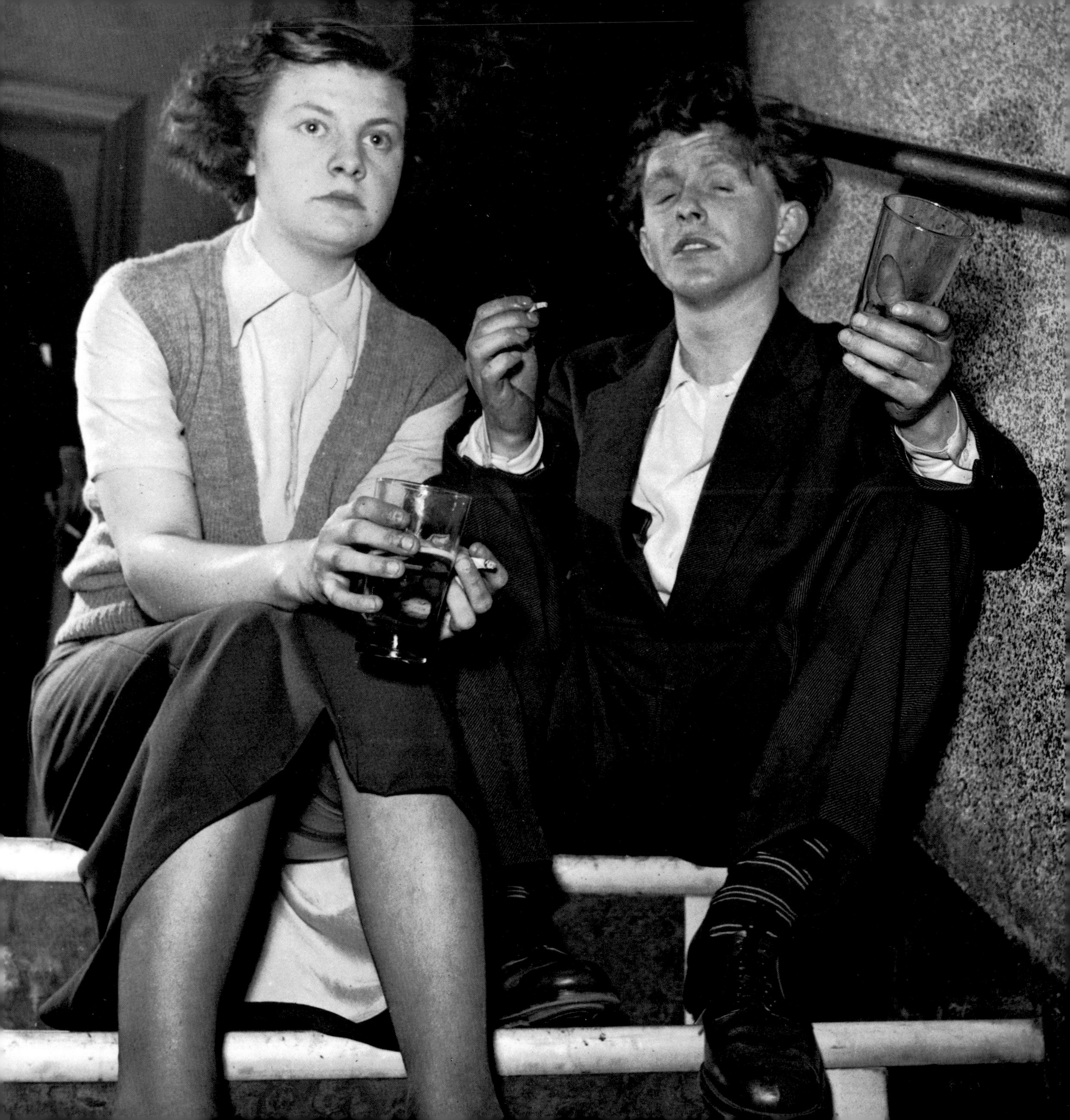

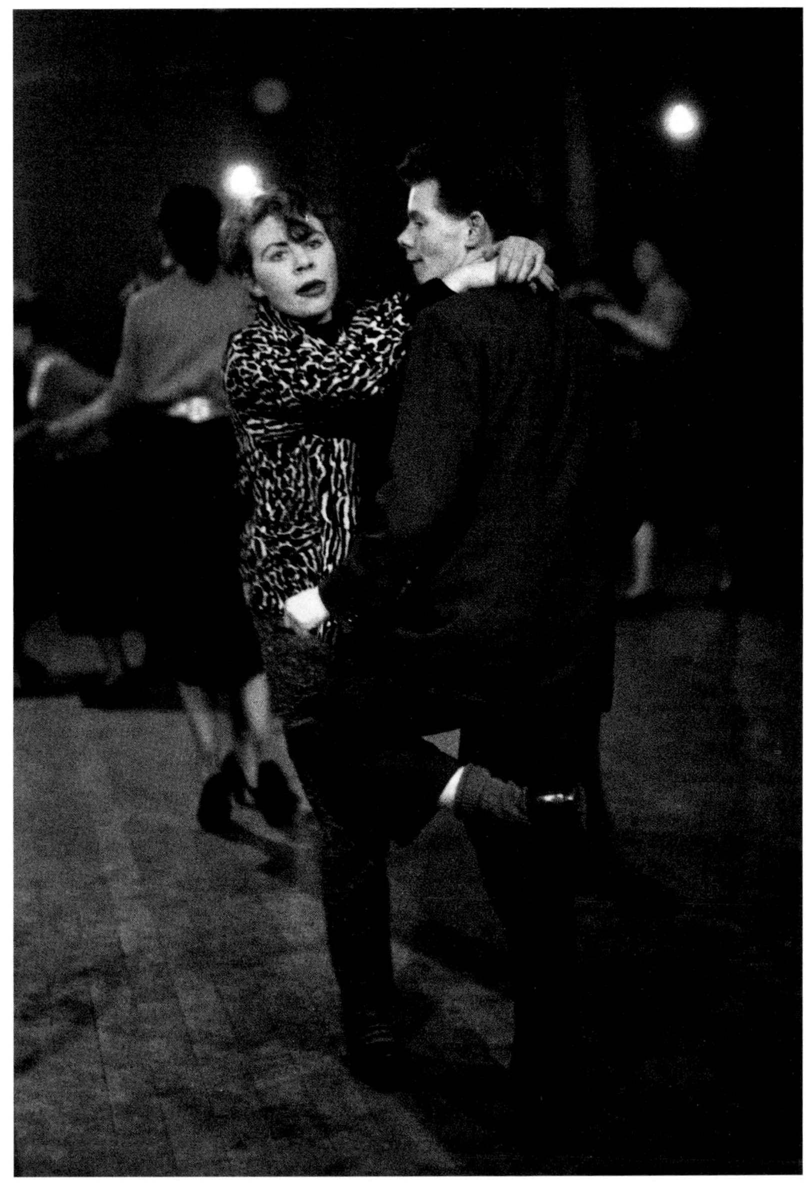

Kurt Hutton
Jazz on Tyneside, *Picture Post, 9 April 1955 (unpublished)*

George Douglas
Jazz Band Ball, Hammersmith Palais, *Picture Post, 7 April 1951*

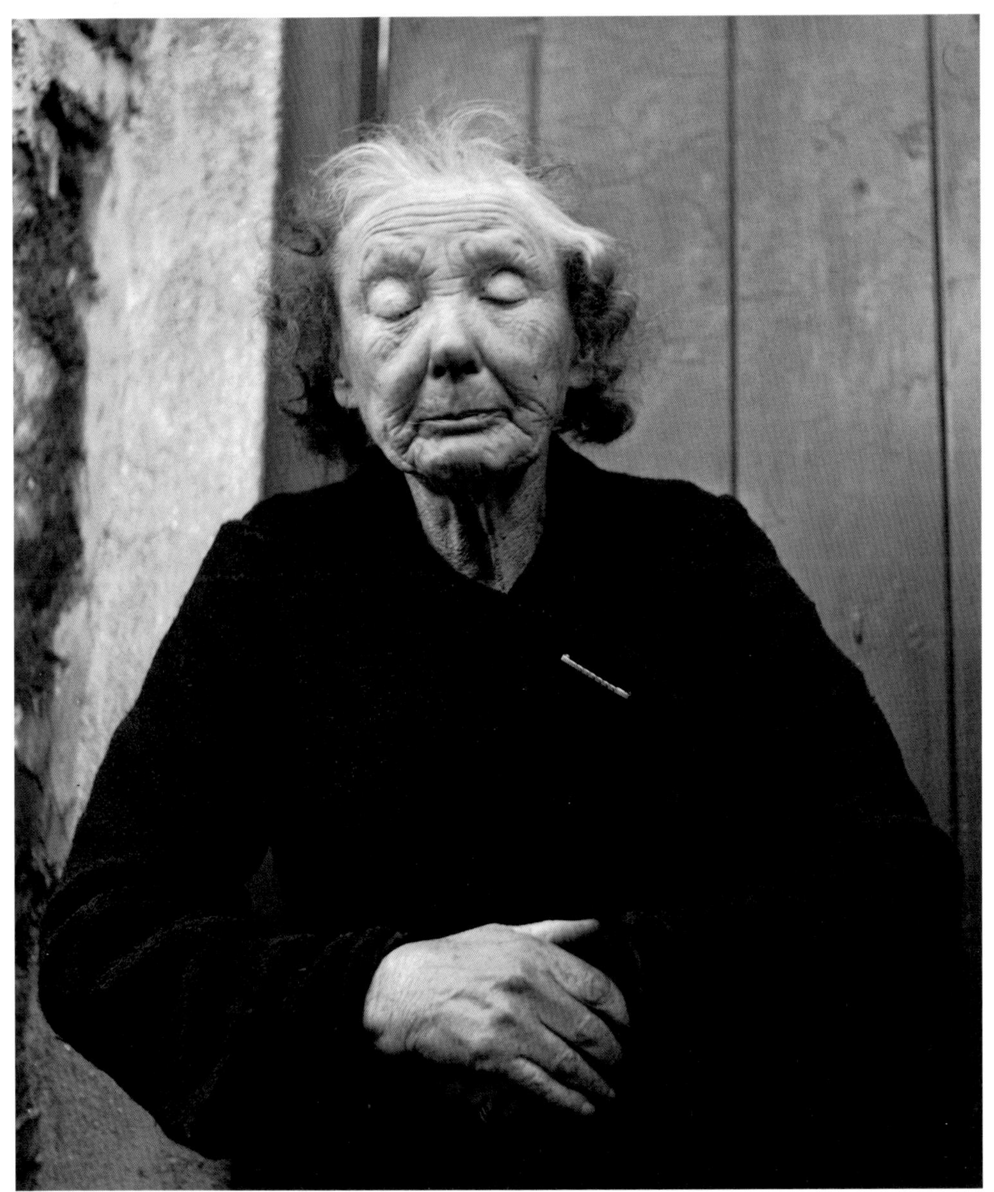

Charles H. Hewitt
The Best and Worst of British Cities, No. 4: Plymouth,
Picture Post, 15 May 1954, (unpublished)
Aged tenant of a condemned house in James Street, Devonport.

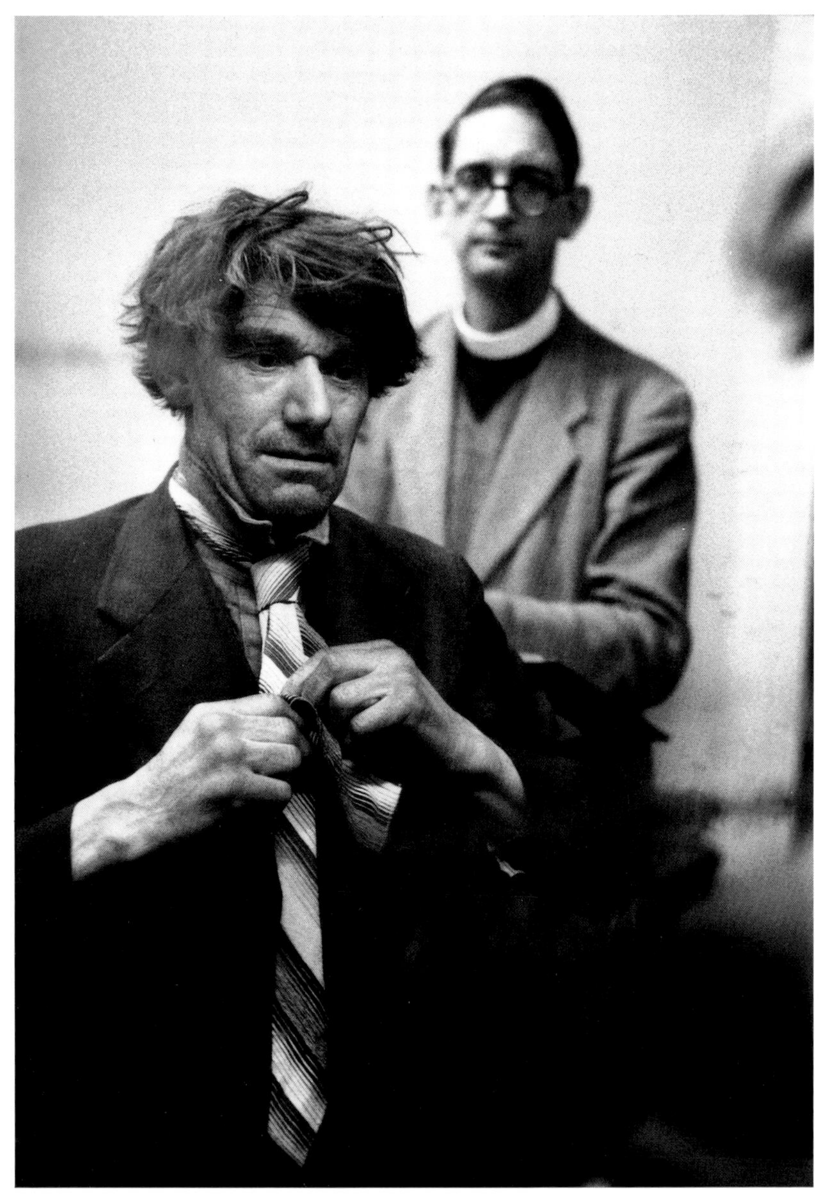

John Chillingworth
St. Georges Crypt, hostel for the homeless, Leeds, *Picture Post,*
1955 (killed story)

Acknowledgements

The Hulton Deutsch Collection

In the Darkroom:
Martyn Austin
Andy Cullen
Brian Doherty
Steve Eason
Donald O'Connor

Conservation:
Leonard Hanson

Negative research:
Derek Brown
Laurence Gillett

Front cover: Photographer unknown, Fox Photos
And it don't seem a day too much, *4 May 1939*
Mr and Mrs William Townsend of Stanton Harcourt
celebrate their golden wedding.

Back cover: Photographer unknown, Topical Press
Waterloo Cup – palatial travelling for Mr. Hales' dogs,
February 1922

Frontispiece: A. H. Robinson, **Berwick-upon-Tweed,
Northumberland – view under bridge from the west**, *1903*